IMPOSTER

Dismantle the stories you tell yourself
and overcome Imposter Syndrome

LAUREN VALBERT

R^ethink

First published in Great Britain in 2022
by Rethink Press (www.rethinkpress.com)

© Copyright Lauren Valbert

All rights reserved. No part of this publication may be reproduced, stored in or introduced into a retrieval system, or transmitted, in any form, or by any means (electronic, mechanical, photocopying, recording or otherwise) without the prior written permission of the publisher.

The right of Lauren Valbert to be identified as the author of this work has been asserted by her in accordance with the Copyright, Designs and Patents Act 1988.

This book is sold subject to the condition that it shall not, by way of trade or otherwise, be lent, resold, hired out, or otherwise circulated without the publisher's prior consent in any form of binding or cover other than that in which it is published and without a similar condition including this condition being imposed on the subsequent purchaser.

Cover image © Shutterstock | Malochka Mikalai

Author photos supplied by Karīna Kaminska

Contents

Introduction — 1
    Do you suffer from Imposter Syndrome? — 4
    Who this book is for — 8
    Who do you think you are? — 8

PART ONE Understanding Imposter Syndrome — 11

1 What Is Imposter Syndrome? — 13
    The four Imposter Syndrome personas — 15
    Short-term Imposter Syndrome — 21

2 What Causes Imposter Syndrome? — 23
    Upbringing — 24
    Childhood environment/school — 28
    The patriarchy — 29
    Country/culture — 32
    Marketing — 33

	Social media	35
	Toxic corporate culture	36
	Education	38
	Introverts in an extrovert's world	40
	The neurotypical world	42
	The good news	44
3	**The Cost Of Imposter Syndrome**	**47**
PART TWO	**Overcoming habitual practices**	**55**
4	**What Are Habitual Practices?**	**57**
	Does it serve you?	59
	Involving others	60
	Coaches and therapists	61
5	**Your Body**	**65**
	Stress hormones	65
	Breathing	66
	Recognising tension	69
	Sleep	71
	Additional resources for body work	73
6	**Your Voice**	**75**
	Your language	78

7	**Your Emotions**	**91**
	Useless emotions	92
	Procrastination	99
	The external judge	103
8	**Your Stories**	**107**
	Feelings of obligation	111
	Sharing your feelings	115
9	**Your Filters And Triggers**	**119**
	Your filters	120
	Your triggers	122

PART THREE Taking Up Space And Exercising Agency   **131**

10	**Dreams And Goals**	**135**
11	**Finding Your People**	**139**
	Activate your fan base	139
	Choosing your family	142
	Making connections	145
	Understanding and dealing with rejection	150
	Decision-making	154
12	**Loving Yourself**	**157**
	Conclusion	**163**

References 167

Further Resources 183

Acknowledgements 187

The Author 191

Introduction

Over the almost three decades I have been working in communications, training and coaching, I have picked up a wealth of experience and knowledge that means I understand people. I have read a fair amount of research studies and books on psychology, but mostly I've just listened to the people around me, in particular to the way they talk about themselves to themselves and others. The way they lied to themselves and others. The way they betrayed their fears, their desires, their beliefs and their blind spots. Their kindness and empathy. Their ability to cope (or lack thereof) and the walls they tried to build around themselves to keep the world at bay.

What I have especially observed is that many people suffer deeply from self-underestimation. A large percentage of those people are women. They are not aware of their skills and talents. They cannot articulate their value to the world. They don't have the courage to try something new, to take a risk, have a dream (let alone a Big Hairy Audacious Goal). They are simply coping and surviving. Doing the thing in front of them. Not even suspecting they have the right to want or ask for more.

When I have worked with these people and asked them, 'Why don't you try something new?' they've look at me in horror and told me, 'I can't do that.' But when I've pushed them and asked why not, their answers have generally been vague. When you have a vague answer to an important question (or no answer at all), it often means you learned this belief when you were too young to understand it. It means it was taught to you against your will and without your consent.

Imposter Syndrome may sound like a big name for a collection of feelings. I use the term 'syndrome' consciously, as it is like an illness with a set of symptoms, an illness that you can 'catch' from a number of sources, though most often in childhood, and it can cause deep mental, emotional and physical damage to sufferers. As with any illness, some people might experience only a mild case that gets better on its own, but there are plenty of people who are suffering terribly. The good news is that there are treatments, even cures. Different treatments may work for different people,

INTRODUCTION

but you can get better and recover from Imposter Syndrome.

I want to assure you that this is not one of those books that says 'You can do anything you set your mind to, and it's easy!' You can't do it all, and you can't do everything you want right away, but you can do a lot more than you think you can. And it's not easy, but it's not impossible and not nearly as bad as your fear and programming make it out to be.

Nor is this a book that confirms your victim role in this journey. If you suffer from any symptoms of Imposter Syndrome, you are a survivor of some shitty teaching and socialisation. You can do a lot to escape the role of victim and regain agency (there is a lot more about agency in the third part of the book). Most importantly, I am not going to confirm your belief that you aren't capable of doing things to change your circumstances. Imposter Syndrome is caused by others, but it can only be cured by you.

I have changed my circumstances, repeatedly, with a lot of help and the crazy belief that trying and failing won't, in fact, kill me. I promise that if you try, and ask for help, you can change your circumstances too.

Even though I have confidence in some areas of my life, I still suffer from Imposter Syndrome in others. In fact, I had a lot of Imposter Syndrome about writing this book and applied some of the techniques

I recommend here to help me through it, so I practise what I preach. I am not always good at doing everything I suggest in this book, consistently or well. I suffer from chronic depression and anxiety, which means I am often too exhausted and stressed to do what I know is best for me. Life often gets in the way of our taking the best care of ourselves.

You should not feel guilty if you can't do everything, or even anything, I suggest. This information is here for you to discover and apply when you can. If your only takeaway from this book is that you are not alone in feeling this way, that is already a step forward. A feeling of isolation and uniqueness (in the worst possible way) are key symptoms of Imposter Syndrome.

Do you suffer from Imposter Syndrome?

As you're reading this book, it's likely that you suspect that you do, but let's help concretise it. What does it mean to feel Imposter Syndrome? You may not have literally thought 'I am an imposter' but have you ever:

- **Felt completely stuck in a situation (business or personal) because you couldn't see a way out?**
  This might be thinking, 'I will never be able to get away from this, it will always be this bad' or 'It won't be any better if I do something different.'
  It can also feel claustrophobic, with physical symptoms such as shallow breathing, heart racing, excessive sweating and feeling faint.

- **Been completely terrified about giving a presentation on a topic you are an expert in, because you were afraid you hadn't prepared enough?** Spoiler alert: When you have Imposter Syndrome, no amount of preparation is enough. It is an excellent idea to practise a presentation, but feeling terrified despite a lot of practice is debilitating.

- **Hated your job but were afraid to even think about what else you could do?** Inertia is a common symptom of Imposter Syndrome, because self-doubt prevents you from contemplating the seemingly impossible number of steps it would take to change jobs or career paths. Again, this can create a terribly debilitating physical stress that can damage your long-term health.

- **Been afraid to ask for a pay rise or promotion because you didn't feel that you deserved it?** This is common: it is estimated that only around 37% of employees in the US have ever asked for a pay rise.[1]

- **Become burned out or ill from taking on too much, because you felt like you had to?** Obligation is closely linked to Imposter Syndrome, often because your parents or caregivers told or showed you that you had to prove you are worthy of love. If you find it impossible to say no without being worried that the person you're saying no to will stop liking you, this is a symptom of Imposter Syndrome.

- **Spent a lot of time worrying about what other people think of you?** This is probably one of the most common human concerns. We are social creatures that want to live in and belong to groups, after all. But there is a difference between wanting to be part of and contribute to a happy group and worrying excessively about what others (especially strangers) think about you, to the point that it affects your mental health. The latter is a symptom of Imposter Syndrome.

- **Read profiles of leaders in your industry, particularly in your demographic, and thought 'I could never do that'?** The press likes to focus on the super high achievers, the people who have done more or are louder than the rest of us. That does not make them more skilled or better at something than you. It makes them more active, but mostly it makes them louder. Not being good at self-promotion does not make you worse than them, it makes you different.

- **Stayed friends with someone toxic because you secretly believed you deserved it?** This has a lot attached to it, not all of which I can cover in one book. I am not a psychologist and would not try to summarise all the reasons why people stay in toxic relationships, but it is a big symptom of Imposter Syndrome.

- **Felt paralysed when someone asked you to 'tell me about yourself'?** Not being able to communicate positive or even factual information about oneself is a classic symptom of Imposter Syndrome, because sufferers tend to focus on the things that are wrong with them, rather than the positives. It also may be that you can answer the question when given time to think about it, but not on the spot. Since we live in a world dominated by self-promoters, not being able to speak up for yourself is often perceived as a weakness.

If the above feelings are familiar to you, it's likely you suffer from Imposter Syndrome. The good news? It's not your fault, and you can get over a lot of it. The bad news? It can be quite hard work and you can't do it alone.

Do you have to do anything about Imposter Syndrome? Of course not. You can live your life exactly as you have, forever. But know that it costs you quite a lot to live like that. In fact, it costs all of us. It silences voices, stifles amazing and creative ideas that would impact the world, and loses us all money, which unfortunately is how many people measure impact.

Who this book is for

This book is for anyone who recognises themselves in the questions above. I have noticed that the people who suffer most, and most often, from Imposter Syndrome are women, minorities and marginalised people. That includes economically disadvantaged people and people with chronic mental or physical illnesses, who of course can be any gender. But anyone can suffer from Imposter Syndrome. Fortunately, anyone can learn how to empower themselves and be more of an advocate for themselves in every aspect of their life.

Though many of the stories I share in this book relate to women, because they are the people I have worked with the most, this isn't a book only for women or AFAB (assigned female at birth) people. I am a cis white woman (who identifies as part of the LGBT+ community and is neurodiverse) and speak from my own experience; I won't try to speak for people in other minority groups or with other mental conditions. That doesn't mean Imposter Syndrome is not a massive problem within those groups – objectively, it is – it just means I can't speak on behalf of those people. Nevertheless, I have tried to include as diverse a group of voices as I can.

Who do you think you are?

'Who do you think you are?' is a question people suffering from Imposter Syndrome often ask themselves, or allow themselves to be asked. It's frequently framed as a negative question, expressing something like, 'How dare you behave like that?' It's often spoken to people (especially women and minorities) who dare to be different, to stand out, to try new things and break the mould. Normally these are the kinds of people that Imposter Syndrome sufferers wish they were more like.

But there is a different way to read this question. Because who we *think* we are *is* who we are. In the most fundamental sense, we create our 'true' self in the way we think about ourselves. We communicate how we feel about ourselves to the world, and that determines how they will look at us and treat us. Not completely, of course, because prejudice exists and we cannot will this away. But we can affect our world by believing in ourselves. Look at Jackie Robinson, Rosa Parks, Malala Yousafzai, Greta Thunberg – each overcame the assumptions of people around them about what they would be capable of, because they believed in themselves. They believed they had a right to exist and express themselves.

In the same way, if you believe that you are terrible at something, guess what happens? Negative thoughts about yourself are a self-fulfilling prophecy. If you think you can't accomplish something, you won't. If you keep yourself small, you will be small. If you allow your weaknesses to defeat you, you will be defeated. You don't owe anyone else a hero's journey with your life, but it would be a shame if you defeated yourself and didn't achieve your purpose.

The exercises in this book are designed to uncover all your programming and the lies you've been taught about yourself, and show you the truth about who you are. When who you *think* you are becomes who you *really* are, you know you have been cured of Imposter Syndrome.

PART ONE
UNDERSTANDING IMPOSTER SYNDROME

Part one of this book is aimed at helping you to understand what Imposter Syndrome is, where it comes from and the various forces underlying and perpetuating it. It will talk about the childhood roots of Imposter Syndrome and the societal and structural forces at work in our adult life that keep us feeling small. You'll discover that you are by no means alone if you're a sufferer of these pervasive conditions.

It will also explain what the cost of all that wasted energy is, personally and for society. We will begin to think about what the journey out of Imposter Syndrome might look like and what resources you can draw on, setting you up for success with the exercises in the later parts of the book.

1
What Is Imposter Syndrome?

Are people born with Imposter Syndrome? No. Babies don't think, 'I wonder if my parents think I'm needy? I bet they hate me.' It is something that we learn and acquire from multiple sources over the course of our lives. Where do we learn it? From whom or what do we acquire it?

Before we think about the sources and causes of Imposter Syndrome, it's necessary to identify the characteristics, or symptoms, of Imposter Syndrome. In what ways might we feel like an imposter in our life? People might identify it differently, depending on their experiences, but I would define it as any or a combination of the following:

- (Excessive) fear of failure
- (Excessive) fear of criticism

- The sense that there is an external judge of one's life, or an external set of criteria one is failing to meet
- Lack of sense of self and an inability to look at oneself objectively
- Lack of confidence in one's own capabilities, even in the face of evidence
- Feeling, secretly or overtly, less than other people
- (Excessive) concern about, and reliance on, what other people think
- A disconnection with a future self specifically, or the future in general
- Black and white thinking (characterised by the tendency to speak in absolutes: 'I will always feel this way', 'It will never get better')
- A feeling that one deserves bad things to happen to them, or that they are not lucky
- Loyalty to the wrong people or things
- A feeling of (excessive) obligation

Some of these may seem commonplace, which is why I clarify 'excessive'. Pretty much everyone has a fear of failure, but if it is paralysing, and stopping you from doing something fun or that will expand your world, it's a problem.

It's also not fully appreciated how many long-term physical problems are caused by Imposter Syndrome.

It puts your body under a tremendous amount of stress, which can result in headaches, cluster headaches, migraines, neck and shoulder pain, back pain, heart palpitations, breathing problems, stomach aches, digestive issues, diarrhoea, and/or muscle cramps.[2] This only adds to the challenges that Imposter Syndrome sufferers face.

You may not recognise all of the above in yourself and you may experience more of these things than others. This will depend on what the specific sources of your Imposter Syndrome were. In the next chapter, I will talk about the many different sources of Imposter Syndrome, but first I'm going to introduce the different ways that Imposter Syndrome can present in people.

The four Imposter Syndrome personas

You may be an Imposter Syndrome sufferer yourself and know others who suffer too, but notice a lot of difference in the way it shows up for each of you. There is no one type of Imposter Syndrome sufferer. Based on my experience and work, I have identified four 'personas'. Which one you are is determined by the sources of your Imposter Syndrome in combination with your unique personality and situation.

In the second and third parts of this book, I will be providing exercises with tips on which persona(s) they're best suited to, so while reading these think about which most closely reflect your own experience of Imposter Syndrome. It's totally possible that you may recognise in yourself traits of multiple personas.

The Introvert

This is probably the most recognisable and familiar of the Imposter Syndrome personas. In general, Introverts understand their own value and skills pretty well (although they may undersell them). Those skills are usually focused on tasks and things they can do in isolation or in small groups. They want and need plenty of time to think, to dive deep, to research, to think again, to prepare, to do some research on the best tools to use to prepare, research and think. Then, and only then, can they talk about or show their ideas. They will take their time, but the end result will likely be perfect and/or beautifully fleshed out.

Their challenge is that they're living in an extrovert's world (more about that in Chapter Two). They experience Imposter Syndrome when they're put on the spot, even in situations when they should be able to flourish.

Introverts:

- Dread being asked 'tell me about yourself'
- Hate meetings that aren't properly mediated because they don't get heard

- Never feel like they've done enough preparation for presentations or public speaking
- Want to get feedback on content, not presentation
- Put up with bad behaviour in the workplace or in personal relationships because they think too deeply and too long about their decision to leave
- Have a hard time acting impulsively
- Tend to do better in one-on-one or small group social situations, rather than big parties or networking events

The Survivor

The Survivor most likely experienced trauma in childhood, such as systemic abuse, neglect, or bullying. They may seem confident in their skills and good at presenting themselves, but in most cases, it's a front. If they get feedback or criticism, they tend to take it personally and get angry or upset quickly and disproportionately. They are often moody and fluctuate between believing that they are everything and that they are total shit, with little in between. They may be diagnosed with one or more mental illnesses or disorders, such as borderline personality disorder, bipolar disorder, post-traumatic stress disorder (PTSD), complex post-traumatic stress disorder (C-PTSD), depression or anxiety.[3/4]

Their challenges are to be able to trust their ability to handle difficult situations, and not to take feedback too personally.

Survivors:

- Tend to use 'black and white' language like, 'It will always be this bad, it will never get better', or 'He hates me'
- Tend to be superstitious and believe in luck
- Believe more often that they haven't achieved 'what they're supposed to' have achieved
- Will be extraordinary when they're 'on' and almost unable to function when they're 'off'
- Are best when judged on results, not on process
- Have trouble with goal setting because they struggle to imagine positive future outcomes

The Eraser

The Eraser likely grew up with parents who suffered from some form of mental illness, or were narcissistic, or who parented in a rigid, controlling way. They were taught to erase themselves, their feelings and their needs in every situation. These are people who are described by others as 'kind', 'easy-going' and 'so helpful', but meanwhile may be dying inside from always putting everyone else's needs before their own. This is the group that struggles the most with what people typically understand Imposter Syndrome to be.

Erasers:

- Struggle with defining their own values, skills, talents and identity
- Suffer the most from overcommitment and burnout
- Suffer the most from obligation
- Stay in bad jobs too long because they feel a misplaced sense of loyalty and/or they don't believe in their ability to get another job
- Stay in bad relationships because of misplaced loyalty or because they think they can change the other person
- Are often in support rather than leadership roles

The Different

These are the people who 'don't fit in'. The largest subset of this group is neurodivergent people: people on the autism spectrum, people with attention deficit disorder (ADD), attention deficit and hyperactivity disorder (ADHD), and/or people with dyslexia. Basically, people whose processing mechanisms mark them out as different from other, 'neurotypical' people.

A Different can also be anyone who grew up feeling dramatically different from other people around them. For example, if a person grows up in a very religious household but doesn't share those beliefs. Also, people who were born in the wrong body or gender, or who suffer from any kind of dysmorphia – where they feel their outside does not match their inside.

These people are often abused or bullied for being different, so they may share some characteristics with the Survivor. But they may also take pride and invest a lot of energy in being different, so feeling different is not always a negative – it's about whether it serves you or not.

Differents:

- Don't always respond well to structure and traditional ways of doing things
- May operate, consciously or unconsciously, as change agents, insisting on presenting different viewpoints or approaches
- May be self-conscious, worried about what other people think of them and obsess about what is 'normal'
- May feel silenced or ignored by neurotypicals
- May have difficulty working in an office, particularly an open plan one, and may need more flexible working conditions and hours

- Can experience a lot of stress or burnout when trying to meet neurotypical standards

The personas are designed to help you observe yourself and identify your particular 'flavour' of Imposter Syndrome, to understand it in more detail. They are not supposed to be restrictive or prescriptive, so if none of these fit you, don't worry. The most important thing is to identify which of the exercises in the later parts of this book will suit you best.

Short-term Imposter Syndrome

There are things that can cause short-term Imposter Syndrome, such as youth or inexperience in a specific area. Or perhaps a serious life event causes you to stumble and doubt yourself, your talents and skills, for example being made redundant or having a long-term relationship end. You shouldn't underestimate the impact of these experiences of Imposter Syndrome, just because they aren't chronic. For example, say you are new to a job and feel insecure; this can set a pattern of behaviour and stress-avoidance that can develop into longer lasting Imposter Syndrome.

You could also find that you feel Imposter Syndrome in some situations and not in others. Having a particular skill set may mean that the work you do in one area makes you feel confident, whereas other types of work do not. Or you may feel confident and capable

IMPOSTER

with some people but not with others. This can be useful to track and investigate, as it will tell you a lot about the source(s) of your Imposter Syndrome, and potentially, what people or situations you will need to prepare more for in advance (as, in many cases, you can't, or shouldn't, avoid them entirely).

It's good to recognise the situations that make you feel 'less than', even if they're temporary. You can use the exercises in the second half of the book to help you get through challenging situations.

2
What Causes Imposter Syndrome?

Now that we know what it is and how it manifests, it's time to discuss where Imposter Syndrome comes from. Growing up, we gather impressions from a wide variety of sources. Depending on the hand that we are dealt in life, many of these impressions can be positive. Unfortunately, some or many of these can be negative and cause us to feel terrible about ourselves. We can take these feelings into adulthood; indeed, they can stay with us for life, reinforcing our self-doubt.

Everyone will experience a mix of influences and it won't be one thing that causes your Imposter Syndrome. Your personality, sensitivity and genetic makeup will all determine how you react to external influences, so two people can have exactly the same background and grow up with differing amounts of self-belief, self-confidence and ability to feel good about themselves.

Some of these factors will apply to you, some won't. The aim of this chapter is not to provide an exhaustive list of people, things and societal forces that cause Imposter Syndrome, it's simply to help you understand that, if you suffer from it, the deck was stacked against you from the start. And also in the middle, and maybe still is now. To become aware of what influences you've been exposed to is to begin to understand your programming. This awareness is the first step toward change.

Many people with Imposter Syndrome blame themselves for it. In this chapter, I want to establish that it is *not your fault*. Your brain has been programmed by people and circumstances out of your control – but it is your responsibility, and yours alone, to recode your brain. I will explain how you do that later in the book. First, let's explore some of the forces that can be at play.

Upbringing

Because our brains are growing and developing all through childhood, the most indelible impressions we form about our self-definition and self-worth are made before we are eighteen.[5] The most difficult to observe, understand and change are the impressions made before we are ten. The people around you during those, your most formative, years contribute hugely to your understanding of yourself. This means it's mostly about your parents/caregivers during that time.

To be clear, I am not saying that it is solely your parents' fault if you have a negative self-image and suffer from Imposter Syndrome, but it is generally true that the less supportive and love-demonstrating your parents are, the more likely you are to have self-doubt in childhood and later in life.[6]

It's difficult to sum up in a few words the effect that parents have on us, because it is so profound. Parents have a thankless job, trying to raise children in a society that judges every choice they make. With the comments below, I am simply giving some examples of ways that parents can have a negative influence on their children and cause them to have self-doubt. This does not necessarily make them bad people, just people who themselves were not shown how to be good parents. Many of them will have been treated in the same way by their own parents, as bad parenting is normally learned from experience.

Some things that parents can do to create self-doubt in children are to:

- Be strict with rules and discipline, not allowing the child freedom to grow in the direction they choose.

- Attempt to force or coerce their child into being just like them, especially when it comes to career or hobbies, for example, 'You should play sports, I loved sports as a child', or 'You should become a doctor like me.'

- Make their love of the child conditional on performance (of chores, at school, in tests, etc), instead of making it clear that they love them no matter what and only want them to do well in life.

- Tell their children repeatedly that they're 'too X' (too loud, too soft, too shy, too aggressive, too fat, too lazy, etc). Parents are responsible for helping children understand rules and limits in a healthy way, but criticising children without assisting them to understand why their behaviour should be different in certain contexts is not helpful. For example, you can tell children, 'You shouldn't shout and run around in a church like you do at home' without making them feel like they are 'too loud' as a defining personality trait.

- Compare their children to each other often, for example, 'Your brother knows how to do it, why can't you figure it out?', or clearly favour one child over another.

- Reinforce, through repeatedly ignoring them or shouting at them, that the things they care about don't matter.

- Try to deny who they are, or make them be something or someone they're not – this is often seen in regard to gender expression or sexual orientation.

Children need to be taught that they matter and that they are worthy of love, no matter what. Those are the most important things for parents and caregivers to teach. Without this, children feel that they are unworthy and that what they want and care about doesn't matter.

I see in adults the effects of having been children of people with chronic mental or physical illness, or with addiction issues. When parents have a lot of noise in their own head, whether from illness or addiction, they can't hear, observe and love their children properly. This forces children to change their behaviour to accommodate the parent(s). Narcissistic or self-absorbed parents have a similar effect on children, forcing them to control themselves and take on responsibility at too young of an age.[7]

Responsibility is a thing children have to grow into over time. If they have to care for their parent, either passively, by adapting their behaviour, or by actively performing caretaker duties, it can make them too focused on and worried about other people more than themselves. This is a common symptom of Imposter Syndrome: believing that others' needs are more important than your own and not prioritising your mental and physical health because you are so busy taking care of others.

More and more people are sharing their stories of childhood trauma. This is hugely beneficial in assisting others who are dealing with the consequences of similar experiences and helps to ensure that no one who has experienced abuse or neglect in their childhood feels alone.

Childhood environment/school

Outside of parents and caregivers, the other major influences in childhood and adolescence are our teachers and peer group.

I moved around a lot as a child. I was also very tall from a young age, and having undiagnosed ADHD made me 'weird', overenthusiastic and hyperactive. All of this inevitably made me a target for bullying. I was bullied from when I was twelve to when I went to college at eighteen; the experience left an indelible mark on me. Bullying by peers can be completely destructive to one's self-confidence and the effects can last long into adulthood.[8]

Many children who are 'different' (which includes practically everyone) are bullied in school, and not only by their peer group. They can be made to feel stupid, freakish, too loud, too soft, untalented or hopeless by teachers too. They can also find teachers who support and believe in them, and who give them a beam of light that they carry with them always. Unfortunately, this is too rare and too random.

In many countries, schools are underfunded and overcrowded, which means teachers tend to reward children that fit the mould of the quiet obedient child over the 'weird' kids who don't learn in a convenient or quiet way, which is often neurodivergent children.

The patriarchy

Yes, I went there. I know it might seem easy to blame larger societal structures, but these things have a direct, daily effect on our lives. To be clear, by 'the patriarchy' I mean the set of standards, norms and rules in societies based on a Judeo-Christian ideology that, explicitly or implicitly, define how and why certain people (typically white, straight men) should be the dominant moral authority and have control of property.[9]

In many countries, patriarchal systems define what individuals in certain demographics are 'supposed' to do and what they are not supposed to do, reinforcing ridiculous, rigid stereotypes for everyone. Men aren't supposed to be nurses. Women aren't supposed to work in construction. Inappropriate constraints are often placed on people because of their gender, race, sexual orientation, and so on. If you have desires to do, be, or act in a different way than the patriarchy has told you that you should, you will meet with criticism and resistance from all manner of sources.

Just look at the way that women are treated in certain fields. Research has shown that women in STEM suffer from tremendous bias, from overt harassment to increased scepticism about their competence and their work.[10] This trend increases dramatically for minority women. One study found that women in STEM felt more isolated from their colleagues, both male and female, and felt pressure to compete for the 'female role' in the team, as it was frequently perceived that there could only be one in a group.[11]

Are women biologically less capable of thinking in a scientific manner? Absolutely not.[12] So what drives the consistent pushback, resistance, hostility and abuse they face in these contexts? Patriarchal concepts of what women 'should do' and what they are 'capable' of.

The patriarchy also expresses itself in more subtle but pervasive ways in society and culture; in a lot of cases, this is cross-cultural. For example, much has been written in recent years about the fact that women are treated differently (read: worse) by the medical field. In disease and medication research, testing is still primarily done on male animals only, meaning that the symptoms or effects experienced by females are often poorly understood, if at all.[13] Diseases primarily affecting women receive significantly less research funding,[14] and women consistently report that their symptoms are disregarded or trivialised when they visit the doctor.[15]

Are women less important to society than men? Obviously not. But we are consistently shown that women's health is less important than men's. What are we supposed to conclude about the way that society views women, given the active and passive discrimination, harassment, neglect and disregard with which they're treated?

The examples I have given above focus on women, as there have been more studies and evidence in recent years that expose the gender bias that seems 'baked in' to many cultures in the world. However, the patriarchy hurts everyone, especially those who are not in the demographic that holds power in that society. That includes minorities, disabled people, and the economically poor.

Codified, bigoted structures in our own social order are amongst the most common and pervasive causes of Imposter Syndrome in adulthood. Because people are defining themselves by rigid societal definitions that fit almost no one, almost everyone ends up feeling different. And in the patriarchy, different equals bad.

Country/culture

The level of Imposter Syndrome, and the types of people who suffer most, can differ a lot from country to country and from culture to culture. For example, I have noticed from my experience that a lot more men seem to suffer from Imposter Syndrome in Europe than in the US, leading me to believe that the social and family programming they receive is different. Another cultural difference is how confident money makes you. In some areas of the world, being well off is not as much of a confidence booster as in others. In addition, subtle things like knowing how to dress well or speak more than one language can also influence how you are perceived in society.

Your cultural background may be driving your Imposter Syndrome more than you're aware of. I know a woman who has spent her whole life in Europe, but comes from a South American background. She feels that the expectations of women in a culture she has never lived in still directly affect the way she perceives herself.

Similarly, some children are subject to almost codified expectations due to their ethnic or cultural background. For example, I know many people from Asian or Jewish cultural backgrounds have experienced extremely rigid expectations of their career choices from their families, no matter where they lived.

It's good to understand the subtle and overt ways that ethnic, cultural, national or regional perceptions affect you, as these beliefs, values and stereotypes may be dramatically affecting your choices, self-expression, and confidence.

Marketing

Modern capitalism began in earnest after World War II. The 1950s in America and in some parts of Europe was a time of unprecedented economic growth and prosperity (mostly for white people), and many people began to have disposable income for the first time in their lives. Companies began to aggressively market products to consumers, and the way to make people want things they'd never had before was to create a need, to make them think they were lacking something. 'You need a washing machine, Mrs Smith. Your neighbours have one, do you want them to think you're poor?'

For seventy-plus years, capitalist marketing has been telling us we're simply not good enough as we are. We are too fat, too pale, our skin is bad, we smell, we're not attractive to the opposite sex, we don't dress well enough. We don't have the right gadgets, the right car, the right watch, the right bag, or the right laptop. Entire magazines exist purely to make women – and, more recently, men – feel bad about themselves. Welcome to the shitty self-image club, gentlemen – ready to start hating yourself?

It's not funny, obviously. Body dysmorphia, eating disorders and other self-image-related issues are on the rise.[16/17] These are exacerbated, directly or indirectly, by being constantly bombarded with images and messages about how we're not good enough as we are. Body issues and eating disorders often co-exist with Imposter Syndrome and, I argue, are directly connected. These types of body issues are, at root, the feeling that you are an imposter in your body and that out there somewhere there exists the perfect body you are supposed to be in but have somehow failed to achieve.[18]

In the April 2022 issue of *Vogue*, Bella Hadid (a woman who many people envy for her looks) talked about her mental illness, Imposter Syndrome and struggles with disordered eating, explaining how she felt that her outwardly 'amazing life' meant that she 'didn't have the right to complain'.[19] Clearly, no one is immune to these connected issues, even, or perhaps especially, those famous for being beautiful. 'There were people online saying, you live this amazing life. So then how can I complain? I always felt that I didn't have the right to complain, which meant that I didn't have the right to get help, which was my first problem.' Does this sound familiar? Put simply: companies make money from making you feel bad about yourself. The marketing they employ to achieve this is a big contributor to Imposter Syndrome.

Social media

> 'Don't let the internet rush you. No one is posting their failures.'
> Wesley Snipes[20]

The twenty-first century saw the emergence of a whole new group of channels through which we could be made to feel inadequate: social media. We have spent the past twenty years scrolling through idealised portrayals of people's lives, making us feel terrible about our own.[21] Social media has been a key factor behind an unprecedented level of depression and suicide amongst teens and young adults in recent years, but many older adults are also in the grip of the disease of comparison.[22] The kind of comparison we engage in on social media has been described as 'comparing other people's outsides to your insides'. This is because very few people post about the shitty parts of their lives. They carefully curate their public image to show themselves at their happiest, their most glamorous, their most successful. If you see these curated personas as the whole story, these people appear better and more successful than you. But it isn't the whole story. These people have had bad things happen to them too, you just won't see any posts about that on Facebook, Instagram or LinkedIn. This is especially true of influencers, who are paid to show a curated version of their lives on social media to sell products.

Toxic corporate culture

The formula of a for-profit company is to create value at the lowest possible price and then sell it at the highest price that the market will bear. The difference between what it costs to create that value and what it can be sold for is the profit margin. If you work for a company, you are a cost and so you need to generate value to offset it. That idea is not inherently bad: we all understand that we cannot expect to receive compensation for no work, we expect to contribute in some way. But over the course of the twentieth century and into the twenty-first, the pressure to increase profit margins has accelerated. This has been caused by several things, but most significantly the stock market and the investment community.[23] What that means for the majority of us is less money for more work. We are expected to deliver more and more, while earnings remain the same or even decrease. It is company employees who end up bearing the brunt of that pressure.[24] Burnout is increasing exponentially, and people are developing stress-related diseases and disorders in record numbers.[25] We are in the middle of what many people are calling 'The Great Resignation' – people are simply leaving jobs they can no longer handle, even if they don't have new jobs lined up.[26]

But there are many people who don't leave jobs that are underpaid and/or causing them physical and mental health issues. Why would a person decide to stay in a job where they are suffering and being treated badly?

WHAT CAUSES IMPOSTER SYNDROME?

This is something I have discussed with many people. In a lot of cases, it seems to come down to two common, yet erroneous, beliefs. First, that you ought to be loyal to the company that has employed you, and second, a belief that you're not good enough to get a job elsewhere, or are too scared to try. Both of these beliefs are rooted in Imposter Syndrome and both are false. You owe a company the best work you are capable of within stated work hours, no more. They are not paying you for loyalty, or overwork, or for making yourself sick. And the skills, talents and experience that are the reasons they pay you, also make you an excellent candidate for jobs elsewhere.

Toxic companies explicitly or implicitly reinforce these false beliefs to keep you from leaving or asking for more.[27] Company leadership, managers and HR people are tasked with making you feel just good enough to function and do your job, but not good enough to ask for a raise, a promotion, more benefits, or a more flexible work arrangement. Leaders and managers are incentivised to discourage discussion amongst employees about salaries and benefits, or God forbid, attempts to unionise.[28] There has been much written about just how much money and time some companies are prepared to spend to prevent workers from organising and/or unionising to improve conditions and benefits.[29]

I'm not saying that every company is toxic. Nor that every manager at a toxic company plays this game.

Additionally, you'll find some toxic managers at good companies. But if anyone at any company has ever made you feel bad for seeking a better situation, or given you harsh criticism without offering assistance or suggestions for improvements, or mocked you, or made you feel bad about yourself, understand that it is on purpose. They want you to feel Imposter Syndrome, so you won't feel empowered enough to demand better, or to leave.

Education

The weight that someone's degree(s) and education is given is also a contributing factor to Imposter Syndrome. In many cultures in North America, Europe and Asia (and probably others, but these I know about), people are expected to have a deep academic background in the field in which they're working, even if that education is out of date or no longer relevant. People are given prestige positions, invited to speak and are cited as experts in their field because of letters after their name, not necessarily because what they say is useful or important.

Higher education is a mark of privilege, even in cultures where education is free. In order to succeed academically, you need to have a safe environment in which to study, enough food to support your brain's ability to learn, money for books and supplies and a family that is supportive of your academic efforts. This means that many intelligent people from disadvantaged backgrounds are not able to access the education and degrees that will allow them to achieve respect, advancement and career opportunities. To focus solely or significantly on the education and/or qualifications a person has been privileged enough to get is to ignore someone's potential.[30]

Research has shown that many people, especially women, will not apply for a job unless they believe themselves to be completely qualified for it. Since a lot of job listings have degree requirements, that means that many people without formal education and/or training that conforms exactly to what is stated in the job description don't apply.[31] This reinforces a lack of diversity in hiring, as the best people for roles may not even apply because they don't 100% fit the job description. Of course, a lack of diversity in applications leads to a lack of diversity in organisations. In the more senior echelons of companies, or in highly technical fields, this effect is compounded.

There will be plenty of people who would dismiss my ability to write a book about Imposter Syndrome, because I do not have a degree in psychology or a related field. Indeed, I am struggling with Imposter Syndrome myself while writing it, questioning whether I am qualified. My response to those people, and myself, is to shrug and say, 'Well, I'm doing it anyway, because I know what I have to say can help people.' I know that I have a lot of experience in understanding people's suffering, irrespective of what the degree I got thirty years ago was in (theatre, by the way). People who don't believe in my ability can read other, more academic books, and I sincerely hope those books help them.

In June 2022, Taylor Swift premiered a video she directed at the Tribeca Film Festival. It was the first time she had directed anything, and she confessed, 'I had this imposter syndrome in my head saying, "No, you don't do that. Other people who went to school do that."'[32] Even a beloved multi-platinum recording artist feels intimidated when she does something for which she does not have the 'correct' qualifications.

I'm glad to say that, in some cultures, the over-emphasis on degrees is beginning to change. The speed at which the world is changing means that, according to the World Economic Forum, '65% of children entering primary school will end up in jobs that don't yet exist.' Many experts predict the future focus will be on 'skilling' or 'reskilling' as we adapt to a changing world, rather than on traditional college degrees.[33] For those of us who didn't know at age eighteen what we wanted to do for the rest of our lives, or who couldn't afford a traditional college degree at all, this change will be refreshing.

Introverts in an extrovert's world

In the ground-breaking book, *Quiet*, Susan Cain explains that between a third and a half of the world population are introverts.[34] But you wouldn't know it from the way the world is run. Extroverts, who thrive on other people's energy and love to be the centre of attention, dominate many spheres of our lives. Parties are extrovert. Meetings are extrovert. Networking events are extrovert. Those dreaded 'team building' exercises are designed by sadist extroverts who truly don't understand why everyone in the room wouldn't want to stand up and talk about themselves.

The majority of introverts I know are left feeling either harassed or left out. It's important not to confuse introversion with being shy. For someone who is introverted, being around other people saps their energy, to varying degrees, so to be pushed into group situations every day is exhausting and challenging. This can find some introverts carefully rationing their remaining energy during the week to avoid burnout, though many end up collapsing every weekend, unable to hang out with friends or engage in hobbies and sports. They can find it hard to keep extrovert friends who don't understand why, if they're 'doing nothing', they can't do something with them.

Many introverts feel bad about being this way, even though they can't help it. I resisted my introverted nature for a long time because I desperately wanted to be the life of the party, even though I couldn't. I experienced serious burnout because I didn't take care of myself and conserve my energy the way I needed to. This is a common experience among introverts.

If you are, or suspect you are, an introvert, there are many reasons to love this about yourself. Introverts often think more deeply, have deeper conversations and love more intensely than extroverts. The introvert's power is in connecting with people one-on-one and finding ways to help others reach their full potential. It is in thinking about problems or ideas so deeply that we can come up with a solution or an opportunity from a completely new angle. We won't be the loudest in the room, but we may be the one who can effect the biggest change, or make the best thing happen.

I strongly suggest that, if you feel exhausted at the end of a work week, if you often feel too tired to do fun things with friends, if even having a good time makes you feel shattered the next day, you consider whether you might be an introvert. This knowledge can help you understand and take better care of yourself.

The neurotypical world

There are many different interpretations of what exactly is meant by the term 'neurodivergent', and varying estimations of how many of us fall into this category. I have seen figures that range from 15% to 30% of the populations of the US, UK and Europe.[35] People with ADHD/ADD, autism/autism spectrum disorder, and dyslexia are widely considered to be the largest groups of neurodivergent people.[36] It's also becoming increasingly common to group those with

C-PTSD and PTSD into this category, as trauma can literally alter your brain function and create sensory processing issues.[37]

Generally, neurodivergence can be understood as a brain processing difference. Those of us who are neurodivergent process the information we receive from our senses in a different way than neurotypicals do. Initially stigmatised and considered less functional, neurodivergent conditions are beginning to be better understood and even gaining appreciation as having certain advantages over so-called 'neurotypicals'.[38] Even so, it still isn't a fun time for neurodivergent people as the world is set up for neurotypicals. From traditional education and learning structures, to social events, public spaces and meeting places, neurotypicals have created a loud, stressful, impression-packed world that is overwhelming for neurodivergents.

This is especially true in the business world. The fact that many organisations expect people to work in an open plan office space five days a week is discriminatory against neurodiverse people. For those of us who have noise issues, or focus issues, or difficulty navigating social interaction, having a desk that is in the middle of people is just hellish. And you know those two-hour meetings? A nightmare for neurodivergents.

The silver lining of the Covid-19 pandemic is that the common myth that everyone has to be in the office every day in order to maximise productivity is now largely disproven. How companies will deal with office time versus home or flexi time is still a developing story, but there is now more flexibility for many people who used to have to go to the office every day. This will create a better and more neurodivergent-friendly work environment over time, which in turn will likely affect social culture too, in as yet undefined ways.

The good news

After all that bad news, there is some good: there has never been a better time to identify, communicate about, and overcome Imposter Syndrome than right now. Over the last couple of decades, there has been a positive explosion of information and resources available to help people deal with mental challenges. As much as media, both mainstream and social, may have contributed to the problem, they're also contributing to the solution. More and more people are sharing their challenges, problems and pain publicly. There are books, TED Talks, videos, discussion groups, workshops, support groups, coaches, specialised therapists and so much more, ready to help. Not only that, the causes of Imposter Syndrome are also being talked about a lot more, and some of them are even changing. The hideous and long-lasting effects of bullying, the link between social media and Imposter Syndrome, the impact of toxic corporate culture, and the stultifying rigidity of the patriarchy are being discussed in more and more public forums.

WHAT CAUSES IMPOSTER SYNDROME?

We have seen how the #metoo movement created a new awareness of and sensitivity to sexual harassment (though it is certainly still happening, with much more still needing to be done). Increasing understanding about the real cost to all of us of Imposter Syndrome (more on this in the next chapter) will continue to make this a popular topic of discussion – and discussion can lead to change.

3
The Cost Of Imposter Syndrome

How can we quantify the cost of Imposter Syndrome? It's difficult even to estimate exactly how many people have it. One of the most common symptoms of Imposter Syndrome is the feeling that you are alone, that you are the only one feeling this way, that talking about your struggles to others will make you seem weak, so you shouldn't do it. This is how Imposter Syndrome maintains and replicates itself, like a virus.

It is important that we understand that most, if not all, humans experience Imposter Syndrome at some point in their life. It seems to be a uniquely human condition, as one must have the metacognition to be able to stand back and observe oneself from another's point of view. This metacognition has given humans the ability to push ourselves beyond all conceivable limits, including of the Earth's atmosphere. It has also given us the ability to judge ourselves harshly.

The ability to observe oneself from an outside perspective can be a good thing. It gives us a necessary distance from our own thoughts, which can be negative, insular and even destructive, because thoughts are governed by emotions, which in turn are influenced by fluctuating hormones and chemicals in our bodies. It helps us to understand when our point of view is wrong, outdated, ill-informed or unhelpful. It can teach us how to communicate better with others who have differing paths and processing abilities to us.

But when we have been taught that we are too much, not enough, wrong, bad, sick or malformed, this capacity for self-observation can be used to criticise, judge, and belittle ourselves. Social media has given us the impression that there are many people out there who are smarter, better, certainly louder, and more capable than we are. We stop ourselves from trying new things, believing in our ideas and speaking up. This leaves us defenceless in a world that is dominated by a comparatively few people who are shouting loudly and drowning the rest of us out.

It is difficult to quantify the effect Imposter Syndrome has had on human progress, because you can't prove a negative. I can't prove that, if everyone had more confidence in their skills, talents and ideas, the world would be a better place. Perhaps it would just be a louder place, with even more people competing for the spotlight. But I don't think that's the case. Much research has been done in the last decade that seems to demonstrate that diverse companies perform better in almost every metric, including profit and performance.[39] 'Environments that encourage diversity and inclusion practices promote trust and employee engagement among employees. Trust in the workplace allows employees to feel secure, reduces turnover, and increases engagement.'[40] The positive results seen in organisations that are focusing on diversity and inclusion are providing proof that hiring people who are different and bring diverse viewpoints, and empowering more people to speak up and believe in themselves, makes an enormous positive difference. It is too early to draw long-term conclusions, but the data we do have is beginning to show that when you create a safe environment for a diverse group of people, those people perform better and more innovatively, which seems a logical conclusion.

Imposter Syndrome sufferers cannot flourish in an environment that doesn't make them feel secure. Research has definitively proven that high-trust organisations that support and positively challenge employees perform substantially better. In addition, employees of these companies report 74% less stress, 50% more productivity, and 40% less burnout.[41] On the flip side, stressed, sick and/or burned-out employees cost companies money – between

$125 and $190 billion a year in the US alone, according to the *Harvard Business Review*.[42] Due to the nature of Imposter Syndrome, sufferers are more likely to develop stress-related illnesses, or become completely burned out. In a survey I conducted on the topic, more than 70% of respondents said they 'often' or 'sometimes' became burned out or ill from taking on too much because they feel like they have to. Over 60% of respondents said that they (sometimes or often) hated their job but stayed because they couldn't think what else they could be doing.[43]

I connect diversity and inclusion in workplaces with those who suffer Imposter Syndrome because 'people who are underrepresented in the workplace can be hit by [Imposter Syndrome] harder' according to a recent *Forbes* article.[44] So, I often highlight research on diversity in workplaces to demonstrate my points, as very little research so far has been done on the impact of Imposter Syndrome on workplaces specifically.

Diversity also directly affects innovation. A study done by *The Guardian* found that 'data shows that publicly traded companies with two-dimensional diversity are 45% more likely than publicly traded companies lacking it to have grown market share in the past 12 months, and 70% more likely to have captured a new market'.[45] Capturing new markets is a key indicator of company innovation and growth, and a homogeneous senior leadership is more likely to miss market opportunities targeting demographics that are not represented in their management.

Imposter Syndrome sufferers are less represented in senior leadership roles and less likely to break into the C-suite. Not because they can't perform in such roles, but because they will not put themselves forward for them. In my survey, I asked how often respondents had been afraid to ask for a raise or a promotion because they weren't sure they deserved it – a majority (78%) said that had happened sometimes or often to them. Although again it is impossible to prove a negative, I believe that those who suffer from Imposter Syndrome are, in general, less successful in business (with success being defined in this case based on salary/money earned, title, promotions and other career opportunities) than those who don't.

I also asked respondents whether they agreed with the following statement: 'I feel like I have missed opportunities in my life because I've been too afraid to take them.' More than 55% said they agreed or strongly agreed. Almost half of respondents agreed or strongly agreed with the statement, 'I feel like I make less money than other people doing the same job at my company', and around 44% agreed or strongly agreed with the statement, 'I have ideas that I think are good but I've been too afraid to talk about them with other people.'[46]

The times, however, are a-changing. One of the only positive outcomes of the pandemic and the subsequent wave of people leaving their jobs has been the fact that companies are now realising that old, outdated employee policies have to change. There has been an enormous increase in the number of organisations offering benefits that focus on employees' mental health, well-being and growth, including more flexible work hours, more options to work at home or other locations, and paying for continuing education, coaching, even therapy. This may be purely because they don't want to lose their workforce, but it is nevertheless a positive development.

The true impact of Imposter Syndrome on our world won't fully be known until we start talking about it and carrying out detailed research, which will allow us to measure the effect. The more sufferers who can get help, either through coaching and therapy, or through online resources, books, videos, podcasts and other resources, the more we as a society will begin to understand the devastating impact it has on our world and, hopefully, we can work together to solve it.

Now that we understand this pervasive and insidious condition known as Imposter Syndrome, and know that the way it makes us feel is not our fault, we must figure out how to lessen and relieve it. No matter what has caused your Imposter Syndrome, despite the fact that it's not your fault you have internalised what you have been taught, told and shown, the only person who can de-program that bullshit and program new, positive beliefs and behaviours, is you. With help, of course, but no one else can reach into you and pull out the things that are holding you back.

So without further ado, let's move on part two, the beginning of the 'action' part of the book that is intended to help you not just understand Imposter Syndrome, but overcome it.

PART TWO
OVERCOMING HABITUAL PRACTICES

In the first part of this book, I discussed how many of the factors that cause Imposter Syndrome are present from childhood. That means we have adapted our bodies and minds to deal with these conditions from a very young age. We are like onions: all of our past selves are still present within us. That means you may now, completely unconsciously, be behaving in ways that served you as a child, but no longer do. The unconscious nature of these behaviours prevents you from observing and changing them. The mind is intrinsically linked to the body, so any sustainable, lasting change must begin with the habitual practices and coping mechanisms we have created, which are often deeply rooted in the body. This includes our voice and linguistic choices, as well as the habitual actions we take (or don't take) and the stories we tell ourselves. To help address this, the first group of exercises I've included in this book are exercises to overcome habitual practices.

PART TWO
OVERCOMING HABITUAL PRACTICES

4
What Are Habitual Practices?

Not all habitual practices are negative. We learn to go to bed when we're tired, eat when we're hungry, clean ourselves when we're dirty. Generally speaking, we don't need reminders to do the basics to keep ourselves alive (severe mental illness aside). However, many habitual practices are energy-draining and do not serve us: 'Doom scrolling' through social media, looking at people who seem much happier than you, thinking, 'That will never be me'; apologising on reflex; avoiding asking for things, so as not to put other people out; judging yourself on where you think you should be and what you should have accomplished by your age. Do any of these behaviours make you feel good? Or are they reflexive, unconscious, habitual behaviours you have learned that make you feel bad?

The exercises in this part of the book are focused on helping you identify any habitual behaviours you have that do not serve you, and may be causing you active harm. These start with identifying how and where you store stress, tension, anger, sadness, or other draining emotions in your body and continue with vocal and linguistic work, because how we communicate is deeply reflective of our mental and emotional state. We'll also take a look at your emotions, which have a tremendous impact on all of our actions and decisions, much more than people suspect, or wish to believe. We will consider the way Imposter Syndrome colours your thoughts and behaviours, from procrastination, to judging yourself against non-existent external criteria, maintaining old stories about yourself, as well as feelings of obligation and not wanting to burden others. Finally, we will talk about two important subjects when it comes to engaging with other people and their words: triggers and filters.

All of the exercises in this book are designed to first, help you become aware of behaviours and thought processes that are caused or influenced by Imposter Syndrome; second, overcome the behaviours and thought processes that do not serve you; and third, redirect and replace habitual behaviours and thought processes linked to Imposter Syndrome with new ways of thinking that *will* serve you, enabling you to take up space and exercise agency.

Does it serve you?

What if some of the behaviours and thought processes that you identify in yourself, that are connected to Imposter Syndrome, actually serve a purpose for you? In conversation with a friend who identified that she definitely uses 'Eraser' language in her communications (see the linguistics chapter for more information on this), I learned that she finds it useful. 'It has been pointed out to me that I do this in work communications,' she said, 'but I use it purposely, as I find people respond to me faster and more positively.' This is a great example of being aware of something that might have been a hindrance and using it mindfully in a way that serves you. With any of the exercises, when you become aware of behaviours or thought processes connected with Imposter Syndrome, if you determine that they benefit you (either generally or in specific situations), by all means continue to use them in this way.

Be conscious, though, that some things can benefit you for a short time but not in the long run. Physical habits, such as carrying stress in your body, can be useful for short-term deadline-oriented gains but will often catch up with you and cause health problems longer term. It's good to periodically check in with yourself, using these exercises to determine if the things that once served you still do, or if it's time for a story update (see the stories chapter).

Involving others

You will not be able to do all this on your own. No matter how self-aware we may be, we are not able to see ourselves fully. If you suffer from Imposter Syndrome, it may be impossible to observe yourself with the love you deserve. A mentor of mine used the metaphor of learning how to do a backwards flip. You cannot do a backwards flip for the first time alone, because your muscles don't know how. You need someone to show you how to do it the first time so that you build the muscle memory to do it yourself.

In some of the exercises, I suggest involving other people. This is so they can provide support, not criticism, constructive or otherwise. Giving useful criticism is more of an expert skill than you may think. It requires the person giving it to be aware of their own filters and to be able to see you clearly. They also need to be good at active listening, to be able to hear and observe what you are communicating with your body language and pick up on the things you are not saying. Imposter Syndrome sufferers are critical of themselves enough, so it's important to ask for help to build yourself and your self-image up, as you may not yet have that skill. Choose your biggest fans to do these exercises with, because they are designed to help you believe in yourself.

Coaches and therapists

If you are having trouble getting to the root of some of the habitual behaviours and thought patterns that are holding you back, I recommend working with a coach who is skilled in active listening and can provide constructive feedback in an objective and informed way. You will know a coach is the right fit for you if they can communicate constructive feedback in a way that feels positive, accurate, and judgement-free.

If difficult feelings and memories come up for you while working through this book, that is normal. I would recommend, in that case, talking to a therapist who is trained to help you process trauma and negative experiences and can treat mental illness. I am often asked about the difference between coaches and therapists. For me, the difference is that coaches are helpful when you have a challenge arising from habitual behaviours and thought patterns and you want an active, directive, solution-oriented partner to help you through it. Coaching usually involves a pre-defined number of sessions, to address one or two known challenges in your personal and/or professional life. There are plenty of coaches with specific focuses on leadership, work communication, personal development, sports and fitness, nutrition, even posture and wardrobe coaching.

Therapy is usually a longer-term process and the therapist typically speaks a lot less. They usually let you identify the problem and dive into it, with some guidance. This is especially important for deep work, when you are working on identifying and healing trauma and issues from childhood. A therapist is carefully trained not to steer or force you to remember, speak about, or process your feelings and memories, as this can warp fragile memories and does not provide valuable insight.

Both coaches and therapists are there to help you build up strength in the areas of life you need support with, especially in the bad times. Imagine life as a river that you're walking through. There will be times when the water is smooth and flowing softly, it's easy to walk in and keep your footing; but there will be times when the current is strong and the water is high, and you will have a hard time staying your course. These are the times when you need help and active support to withstand the strong current.

There are interconnected areas of active support:

- Your assigned family
- Your chosen family
- Your belief in yourself

Your chosen family is distinct from your assigned family, which are those people you are related to by birth, or grew up with from childhood. Your chosen family are the people in your life that are closest to you, the people you would depend on in an emergency, as opposed to more casual friends who you don't necessarily depend on.

Like the sides of a triangle, these areas of support are strongest when they're all in place and connected. When one (or more) of these areas is weak or underdeveloped, you are less likely to be able to withstand the high water moments of your life. If it's not possible to have three strong areas (for example, if your assigned family is abusive or unsupportive), you will need to lean on the other two even more to support you.

Generally, coaches are there to help you develop belief in yourself. They may also help you strengthen relationships with your chosen family. Therapists can help you with all three areas, but are especially useful when it comes to processing feelings and memories about your assigned family and strengthening relationships with assigned family members, if that's a desired outcome.

5
Your Body

Your body is with you all your life. You may love your body or hate it; love some parts but not others; compare it; treat it well or treat it badly. No matter what we do, our bodies are there for us. They keep a record of all the choices we make in our lives, and everything that happens to us leaves an imprint. This is especially true of trauma and stress.[47]

Stress hormones

We all carry stress in our bodies and must consciously release it before those muscles and body parts can relax. The reason is that, when we are put under stress, our body releases two hormones: adrenaline and cortisol. These hormones are designed to 'power up' the body to engage in a fight-or-flight response. They raise your heart rate, shorten your breath, pump blood into your muscles and sharpen your vision. But their effects are intended to be short-lived and burn off as you respond to the outside threat, by fighting or running.[48]

Adrenaline automatically dissipates and leaves your system, leaving you feeling shaky and nauseated, but cortisol doesn't – on the contrary, it will continue to build for as long as you feel stressed.[49] Each of us is carrying unnecessary cortisol in our systems at various points. Cortisol only leaves your body when you do something to release it, whether that's by swearing loudly, exercising, taking a brisk walk, or venting/talking to someone who will listen.[50] You may have heard of primal scream therapy; it was developed to release cortisol – though it's perhaps not practical in an office setting.

Breathing

As I mentioned above, when triggered by stressful situations, your body will automatically shorten your breath. This mean that, when you are nervous or stressed, you will stop filling your lungs with oxygen; instead, you will take rapid, short breaths designed to pump the muscles with blood to prepare them to run. This change in breathing cycle is triggered by the amygdala, the 'fight-or-flight' part of the brain, but once the cycle of short breaths begins, this tells the rest of your body that something bad is happening, which reinforces the feeling of nervousness and panic all over your body.[51]

When you feel nervous or stressed, an effective way to quickly tell your body that you are not in a life-threatening situation is to practise deep breathing. This is a conscious counteracting activity. Focusing on lengthening and slowing down your breathing and filling your lungs completely will work to counteract your body's belief that it is in a life-threatening situation and you will feel calmer.

When I first tell people to fill their lungs completely, they tend to puff their chest out, but this doesn't help as much as you might think. Instead, concentrate on a spot about two inches below your belly button and think about breathing into that spot, expanding and pushing out your abdomen. This will fill your lungs more deeply than pushing out your chest. You should feel the effect after only a minute or two of breathing into your abdomen, but try to do it for five to ten minutes at a time; this will help your body understand that it is safe and can relax.

The reason why breathing is so important when you are feeling the symptoms of Imposter Syndrome is that it is closely linked to your mental state in a given moment. Think of a time when you were called on in class, or asked to stand up and speak in front of a group at work without preparation, or invited to 'tell me about yourself' at a networking event or job interview. You are fearful of making a mistake or being judged, of being exposed as a failure in front of your peers or an authority, and as you panic, your amygdala is triggered and thinks this is a life-or-death situation. It *feels* like it is, even though it isn't. The first thing you need to get a handle on is that automatic panic response.

EXERCISE: BREATHING

Good for all personas

When you are already relaxed, practise deepening your breath a few times. Place your hand on your abdomen below your belly button and practise pushing your hand out with your breath. Do this for at least 5–10 minutes at a time. If it helps, close your eyes while you do this and focus on the spot where your hand is.

Then, the next time you are put on the spot in a meeting or other situation and you feel your heart racing and your breath shorten, as soon as you can afterwards step into the bathroom or other private space and practise the same breathing technique, again for as long as possible.

After a while, you may be able to recognise in the moment when your body is triggering this response and can change your breathing in that moment. Even if you can't use your hand as a guide or close your eyes, you can breathe deeper and counteract your body's impulse to shorten your breath. With practice, this gets easier and easier.

Recognising tension

In the fight-or-flight response, the body tenses up, usually in specific places. You may not be aware of those parts of the body tensing at the time, but you can feel it afterwards. In a lot of cases, if the cortisol is not released you will continue to hold tension in those parts of your body and they can become long-term trouble spots.

Examples of places where people hold tension without being aware of it include the muscles in the head, particularly the forehead and the jaw, the neck, shoulders, upper back, middle back, lower back, hands, forearms, stomach, thighs, calves and the feet. Interestingly, people will hold tension in different spots, often because of physical behaviours learned from childhood: for example, people who needed glasses in childhood often get tension headaches in their forehead, temples or around the eyes and may still squint when they get tense, even if they're wearing corrective lenses now.

Common places to hold tension are the neck, shoulders and upper back, because many people sit hunched over a computer for eight or more hours a day.[52] You're already putting your body under tension in those areas, so your body will automatically tense there as a stress response.[53] Another sign of tension in the body is fidgeting with your hands. This can range from wringing your hands, to tapping or flicking your fingers, fiddling with jewellery, or biting your nails/cuticles. This is one expression of 'stimming' as well, a common characteristic of people with ASD or ADHD.[54]

A note about the physical exercise below: As with any physical exercise, only undertake what is appropriate for you.

EXERCISE: FINDING AND RELEASING TENSION

Good for all personas

The first important step is to become aware of where you hold tension. When you've had a stressful day or week, where do you feel pain? Do you get headaches (not related to known medical conditions)? Neck aches? Back pain? Where in your back? Or are your hands, arms or legs sore?

Once you become aware of where you hold tension, find exercises that help you relax those parts of your body. Just simple exercises that stretch your neck, shoulders, back, arms or legs. You could ask a doctor or physiotherapist for suggestions. Practise doing these on a regular basis, even when you aren't feeling pain, as a conscious counteracting activity. Daily is best, perhaps before you go to sleep.

Once you have a few familiar exercises, try using these throughout your day, in moments when you might feel stress or pain. Many organisations are happy for their employees to take stretch breaks.

Next, become aware of any nervous tics, such as tapping, fidgeting with jewellery, biting your nails.

If these are stimming activities that release stress, then continue to do them, but understand why and when you do them. Are they conscious ways to help you release stress in the moment, or are they needless distractions? If you notice that they come from nervousness, try the breathing and stretching activities instead. These will relax you more than fidgeting will – a clear sign that your body has nervous energy it needs to burn.

Sleep

Sleep is enormously important to your mental and physical health. It seems like every week there is another article about the amount and quality of sleep you should be getting – and probably aren't. Maybe you feel guilty or stressed about the amount of sleep you're getting. Feeling guilty or stressed about it can actually make you sleep less, so you might feel trapped in a vicious cycle.

Imposter Syndrome is often associated with problems sleeping. Overwork and obligation can prevent you from going to sleep at a good time, or from sleeping as long as you need. You could lie awake for hours thinking about mistakes you may have made, or worrying excessively about what other people think of you. The result is that you sleep poorly and/or don't get the amount of sleep your body needs.

It's hard to provide a cure for difficulty sleeping, or insomnia. I suffered for many years with terrible sleep and it was only through intensive therapy that I was able to get over it. But there are habits you can adopt that can help, depending on the cause of your sleep problems, including creating a regular and consistent bedtime, switching off screens at least an hour before you want to fall asleep, and using meditation and breathing techniques such as *yoga nidra* (there are a lot of guided *yoga nidra* meditations on YouTube).

The exercise below is one I've given to many of my coaching clients and friends, all of whom have found that it helps. It's not a new idea and its positive effect has been confirmed in research.[55]

EXERCISE: JOURNALING

Good for all personas

If you have difficulty with busy, intrusive or negative thoughts preventing you from falling asleep, keep a journal or notebook by the bed. Right before you turn out the lights, write down everything that's on your mind. Whether it's good, bad, logical or nonsensical, just do a full brain dump of all the things swirling in your mind. Then, try to go to sleep. If thoughts start intruding again, sit up and write them down. Repeat until your mind feels empty.

If you are the kind of person who wakes up in the middle of the night, you can do this every time you wake up (if you sleep with a partner, it is probably a good idea to invest in a book light). A lot of people struggle with '3am thoughts', which always seem to be a delightful patchwork of our worst-case scenarios and fears. Write everything down and try not to re-read it straight away. It isn't supposed to make sense, it's just to get it out of your head.

Some people tell me they're afraid to write down negative thoughts as it may 'make them seem truer'. In general, I find the opposite happens. Often when you later read what you wrote in a moment of fear, you can clearly see that it's nonsense, and it can help reinforce the fact that the fears your brain dreams up in the middle of night are mostly overblown and unrealistic in the light of day.

Additional resources for body work

There are a lot of resources you can use for body work and improving the way you release stress. Practising yoga on a regular basis is a fantastic way to learn where you hold tension in your body, as well as how breathing techniques can lower and release stress.

Meditation is also an excellent way to practise breathing techniques and become aware of tension in the body, nervous tics and other physical habits. There are many books, videos and classes about meditation and I recommend working on implementing some sort of meditation practice in your routine if you can. There are also specific workshops focused on guided breathing that can help a lot with anxiety.[56]

For people with chronic mental or physical illness or limiting conditions, Spoon Theory is a fantastic resource.[57] It was developed by Christine Miserandino in 2003 to explain to a friend how it felt to have the chronic illness lupus. It is based on a metaphor that describes the amount of mental or physical energy a person has available for daily activities and tasks, and is an extraordinarily simple, non-judgemental way to assess your body's ability to achieve the tasks you're asking it to perform in a day. It is also an excellent way to explain your limited energy and ability to perform tasks that others take for granted.

6
Your Voice

Your voice is your power. Using your voice, its tone, strength and volume, enables you to communicate a tremendous amount – even if someone doesn't speak the same language. Your voice is an instrument and you can use it to fill a room, or speak so quietly that the person sitting next to you can't hear it. After body language, it is the thing that people notice and remember the most about your communication.

Many people with Imposter Syndrome have trouble speaking up in certain situations. Speaking, unless your words are carefully prepared and memorised, is a form of improvisation. People will judge your volume, your intonation, the emotion with which you speak and your word choice. People will look at you with the expectation that what you say should matter, should carry weight, should inform them, should inspire change. It puts you on the spot. Or at least, that is the perception that many unconfident people have. In truth, many people are not listening to you at all; they don't care what you have to say and are too bound up in their own head to hear what's in yours.

Every situation in which you have to communicate is different, so it's hard to generalise. There will be times when you will have to speak and be judged. There will be times when the stakes are low and people won't really be listening to you. In your mind, though, it may carry the same weight – this is a common symptom of Imposter Syndrome. So why speak? We learned in the first part of this book about the cost of Imposter Syndrome. People's fear of using their voice has led to a few loud voices dominating the global/local/organisational conversation. You should speak because you are in the room for a reason. You have a unique set of experiences, impressions, skills, talents, and mental and emotional understandings. There is no one in the conversation like you. No one can replicate the set of circumstances that makes you unique. Add your voice to the conversation because by doing so, you enrich it.

The best way to get over the fear of speaking is to do it. Like any kind of instrument, you'll get better at using your voice with practice. You can change quite a bit about your voice through a few simple vocal exercises. These exercises may make you feel extremely self-conscious. Observe where in your body you feel that self-consciousness, where you are holding onto the belief that your voice shouldn't be heard. As you do the vocal exercises, focus on relaxing these parts of your body.

EXERCISE: SPEAKING

Especially good for Introverts and Erasers

Write down a list of your favourite things about yourself. They can be personality traits, professional traits, interpersonal traits, even physical traits. Try to come up with at least ten things. (If you cannot come up with ten, skip ahead to the fan base exercise and get your friends/family to help you come up with your list.) Craft the list so that you begin each item with 'I', so, 'I am smart', 'I am kind', 'I am a loyal friend', 'I have nice eyes', and so on.

Next, stand in front of a mirror, about 5 feet away, positioned so that you can see at least your head and shoulders. If you have body image issues, do not use a full-length mirror. I want you to concentrate on your face, not your body. Read your list out loud, looking at yourself in the mirror. Feel silly? Great. Do it again. Do it at least ten times, trying as much as possible to look yourself in the eyes as you do it.

Now back up another 5 feet and read through the list again, speaking louder this time. Pretend that your reflection is someone across a crowded room whose attention you're trying to catch. Speak louder each time you read the list, until it makes you uncomfortable and concerned that the neighbours will hear. Then do it again once more at that volume.

Next come the silly voices. Try reading the list at a higher pitch. Try reading it using as low a voice as you can. A tip to speak lower is to imagine you're speaking from your belly. Try to sound like James Earl Jones saying, 'This is CNN'.[58]

Try it with any accents that you can do, still maintaining eye contact with yourself and trying not to laugh. Then I want you to stand tall and read the list again in the softest voice you can, while staying 5 feet back from the mirror. Speak so softly that you can barely hear yourself. Then increase your volume little by little. Try to find the volume you feel most comfortable speaking at and practise at that volume a few times. (By now, you should have the list memorised.)

Finally, I want you to ask someone who loves you to stand 10 feet away from you and listen to you read the list. Ask them what they think of your volume. Can they hear you? I bet they want you to speak louder. Try it a little louder. Keep going until they can hear you comfortably. Remember how this feels. This is your new speaking volume when you are in a group conversation. Practise speaking at this volume in situations where you feel comfortable, because this is the volume you deserve to be speaking at in all situations.

Your language

We've focused above on the vocal component of your communication. How you can use your voice as an instrument to communicate to others your thoughts, ideas, passion, skills, talents, hopes, dreams and the things that make you unique. Now let's turn our focus to the way you say things. Everyone has their own vocabulary, which can be as different as our personal style in other areas. But there are two sets of common linguistic phrases that pretty much everyone with Imposter Syndrome uses; it marks those people out like they're wearing a uniform of self-doubt. I call those two sets of phrases the 'SuperEgo Parent' and the 'Eraser'.

The SuperEgo Parent

The super ego is a concept developed by Freud as part of his ground-breaking work on understanding the various roles of different parts of the mind. For those not familiar with Freud's writings, he theorised that the super ego is a controlling part of the human psyche that tells us we must do certain things. Many people with Imposter Syndrome feel a sense of having to shame themselves into doing the 'right' things, because they've been convinced that their natural instinct is to be bad, wrong and lazy. The child within us is always listening, and they hear when you speak badly of yourself or say harmful things. The language of 'The SuperEgo Parent' sounds like: 'I have to' and 'I should'. Everyone says these things from time to time, but if you listen to people with Imposter Syndrome, they say stuff like this *all the time*. Everything becomes an obligation and they push themselves from mandatory task to mandatory task, feeling guilty and ashamed of the small voice inside that says, 'But I don't want to do that'. It becomes a life of obligation – at work, at home, with friends (how many times have you thought 'Urgh, I don't have the energy to go to the party, but I have to or they'll be upset'?), with hobbies, with everything. These people burn out because they don't know to alternate doing things that they *have* to do with doing things they *want* to do (which can include doing *nothing at all*).

There is a darker tone to the SuperEgo Parent. When you make a mistake, do you say to yourself, 'What an idiot'? Do you call yourself names and tell yourself how stupid you are? This is a particularly destructive trait of the SuperEgo Parent; quite often, it is the internalised voice of an actual parent. Remember that all of your past selves are still inside you, and when you talk to yourself like that, with such negative language, you are speaking to your inner child. The effect is of programming your brain to think it's stupid, rather than of preventing future mistakes.

The Eraser

The SuperEgo Parent is often how people with Imposter Syndrome talk to themselves; the Eraser is how they speak to others – using language that erases their own personality, opinions, desires, or power from their speech. This can be something as innocuous as saying, 'It's only me' when you walk through the door, to starting every statement with, 'It's probably not important, but I think…' Or it might be allowing yourself to be interrupted or talked over. This shows that you have been trained to erase any objectionable part of your presence.

A quick sidenote: I know that allowing yourself to be interrupted or talked over is a difficult thing to overcome if you are in an environment that listens to, reinforces and encourages some voices over others. But this is changing – too slowly, but it is – and good meeting leaders will help ensure that your ideas and opinions are heard. Still, this is somewhat difficult, at times impossible, to control.

When I am in situations where I am tempted to erase myself, I like to think of those who have refused to be silenced when others have tried to shut them down or speak over them. Elizabeth Warren, who nevertheless persisted;[59] Maxine Waters reclaiming her time;[60] Greta Thunberg, who scolded a roomful of adults aged just sixteen.[61] Even if those inspirational role models can't change what's happening in the room at that moment, those examples remind me that I'm not alone in being talked over. Eraser language will not help you to be heard – it is far easier to speak over a person who is already removing themselves from the conversation.

For the linguistics exercises that follow, it is vital that you are able to listen to yourself without judgement. When you're listening with judgement, after you've spoken you might think something like, 'Urgh, that was a stupid thing to say', or, 'I shouldn't have said that, now people will think I can't do my job.'

To practise listening without judgement, instead of putting a negative value on something you have said, ask yourself, 'Why did I say that? Was I nervous? Did I feel pressured to speak? Why is this person's opinion important to me?' Approaching the situation with an inquiring mind allows you to view it more objectively, from a distance. You can only become aware of – and change – your linguistic patterns when you can view your speech as objectively as possible.

EXERCISE: OVERCOMING THE SUPEREGO PARENT

Especially good for Survivors and Erasers

The first exercise will help you to overcome SuperEgo Parent tendencies. The first step is to listen for when you say the following types of phrases:

- I have to...
- I really should...
- I must...
- I feel obliged to...

How often do you use these phrases? When you use them, do you feel tired and lacking in energy? Do you wake up already exhausted, knowing that your day will be full of 'have-to' chores?

Try replacing those phrases with the following:

- I want to...
- I could...
- It's possible for me to...
- I'm excited to...

This may feel weird and artificial at first, but keep trying to actively interrupt yourself when you use one of the first group of phrases and replace it with something from the second. Does it change how you're feeling about the thing you're about to do? Does it help your mood? It may not immediately, or always, but if you can shift your thinking so that you're volunteering for or choosing to do things instead of being forced to, it teaches your brain to have agency. There will be things you're required to do, every day, but if you can frame this as a choice, you will feel more positive about it.

For example, there may be a project that you are working on tasks for. You have to get those tasks done before Monday and it's now Friday morning. Instead of thinking, 'I *have* to do those things before Monday', try telling yourself, 'I'd really like to get those tasks done today, so I can have a relaxing weekend.' Now you've given yourself the choice to get them done, with a reward in the form of a relaxing weekend. If you can manage to do that for your weekend self, just think how grateful and happy that self will be.

One of the reasons that you might be using so much SuperEgo language is if you have a long list of things you have to do. Most people have too much on their plate. In this context, it's easy to see the hours between when you wake up and when you go to bed at night (and maybe don't sleep because you're thinking about all the things that you still haven't done) as a sequence of 'have-to' demands. As I've mentioned, we contain all of our past selves within us, including the child we once were. Can you imagine telling a child, 'Here is a list of things you have to do today – you've got to do all of them, there's no time to play'? Of course not. We don't expect that from children. Why do we think we can do it to ourselves? Adults need rewards and breaks too.

EXERCISE: REWARDS AND BREAKS ACTIVITIES

Write down a list of all the things you have to do today, including both work and personal tasks. Look for three or four items that can be postponed to tomorrow, or another day, and replace them with three or four fun activities. Perhaps things like eating your lunch outside with friends, or by yourself quietly; taking a break to watch a funny YouTube video; when working from home, having a five-minute dancing break where you put on a good dance tune, turn it up loud and move your body; going for a walk outside; spending quality time with a pet; making a quick phone call to a friend. None of these take more than a few minutes out of your day, but they provide a break from the relentless 'have to, have to, have to' in your day. By substituting things that were on your list, not adding to it, you're not giving yourself any more to do in your day.

Similarly, think about how you speak to yourself – and then imagine saying those things to your eight-year-old self, for example. Would you be so harsh?

EXERCISE: TALKING TO YOUR INNER CHILD

If you often speak to yourself in negative or denigrating terms, start paying attention to *when* you do that. Observe your reaction when you make a mistake. For example, if you forget your keys and say to yourself, 'What a stupid idiot I am.' In that moment, imagine instead that you're saying those words to a child. Your child, a child in your family, or the child of a friend. Imagine that they made a harmless mistake and you looked them right in the eye and said, 'What a stupid idiot you are.' How would that feel to say? How would they feel hearing it? It would likely feel awful on both counts.

Now when you catch yourself criticising and/or insulting yourself like that, try making a factual or positive future statement about the situation instead. For example, 'I forgot my keys', or 'I'm going to try and put my keys in the same place so that I remember to grab them.'

Apologising or using softening language before you express yourself comes from either fear or disbelief in yourself, or both. Fear comes from being exposed to the negative consequences of expressing yourself in an unsafe space. If you were told or shown that your opinions and knowledge aren't important, you will be afraid of expressing yourself, even as an adult.

EXERCISE: ERASING THE ERASER

Watch for when you use 'qualifying language', whether in your written or verbal communication with other people. Qualifying language looks like:

- 'Maybe it's just my opinion, but...'
- 'Sorry, but...'
- 'Am I the only one in feeling that...'
- 'I think that [before a fact]'
- 'I feel that [before a fact]'
- 'Maybe it's not important, but I wanted to add...'
- 'Maybe we should try...'

Disbelief in yourself can develop at any point in your life and may be specifically tied to your career, the job you're currently in, or even just a part of that job. For example, you may be brilliant and forceful in presenting data you have gathered, but when it comes to analysing and extrapolating that data to come up with a conclusion, you may panic. Or you may be confident with your team, but easily feel flustered in other groups.

It is important to identify *when* you use qualifying language to determine what situations make you feel like it is not safe enough and/or you are not smart enough to express yourself confidently.

As well as specific settings, are there particular types of people that you use this language around? Are the people you feel nervous around people who tend to interrupt, or who are overly critical of others, or who are obviously not listening to you? Write a list of characteristics of the type of people who make you feel nervous or afraid. This way, if you know you're going to encounter people like this, you can prepare yourself using the breathing and vocal exercises provided in this book.

The next step is to replace qualifying language with 'bridging language'. This is language that invites other people into the discussion, rather than speaking aggressively. Example phrases might be:

- 'Shall we discuss...?'
- 'Is it possible that we could...?'
- 'Could I ask...?'
- 'Can I bring up...?'
- 'I'd like to add...'
- 'I'm going to jump in here and say...' (particularly useful when trying to speak during an active discussion)
- 'I think it'd be useful to redirect the conversation to...'
- 'Let's try it this way and see what happens...'

Bridging language is especially useful in tense situations (whether just for you, or for everybody), such as negotiations.

One you've got comfortable with using bridging language, practise using straightforward language, starting with situations where you feel okay about expressing yourself directly. Straightforward language is similar to the above, but without the qualifiers, so not prefacing your statements. Examples might be:

- Simple statements like, 'We need to do X', 'We're going to try it this way.'
- Only using 'I think' or 'I feel' when you are expressing an opinion, never a fact.

- Leading with facts, even saying, 'The fact is...' to let people know something is not up for debate.
- Speaking up when you have more knowledge than the people talking, for example, 'From my experience as a data scientist, this is not a helpful discussion to have without data.'

I want to add a special note about excessive apologising. If you are a person who apologises a lot, listen to yourself and identify what situations you are reflexively saying sorry in. Have you genuinely harmed, wronged or upset another person? Or are you apologising for your presence in the room, for having an opinion, for taking up space?

Excessive apologising is a learned behaviour. It is learned from people and situations that taught you that your existence was inconvenient. Don't be sorry for being sorry. Be *angry* that you've been taught to feel sorry for being you. Every time you hear yourself apologising, stop. When you're with people you trust, ask them to help by pointing out when you reflexively apologise. Find other words to substitute for those words, like, 'If I may' or, 'Can I?' These are more like bridging language than qualifying language, and make it more polite than apologetic, which is a step in the right direction.

I avoid being directive in this book, but this is an exception. It is very important that you recognise and remove excessively apologetic language from your vocabulary. You teach other people how to treat you; if you are apologising all the time, it teaches people to treat you like a mistake. You aren't a mistake. Take up the space that's yours.

7
Your Emotions

Whole books have been written about emotions, their causes and how we use and misuse emotions to understand and shape our world. In the first part of this book, I talked about how emotions can be shaped by early experiences and how emotional memories from our past can cause us to react negatively to things that happen in our present.

It is good to remember that emotions are primarily caused by a mix of our past experiences, hormones, and the context of what's happening in the present. Everyone has hormonal fluctuations; levels can be affected by the amount of sleep we've had, our diet, physical activity and stress level, among other things. A damaging gender stereotype is that 'women are emotional', but absolutely everyone can and will have wildly fluctuating hormones at various points in the day, week, month that affect their mood.

Your emotions can also be affected by things outside your immediate environment. Much has been written about the psychological effect of the pandemic and global lockdowns, for example. That kind of global event can colour your mood, even if it's not having any impact on your life directly in the present. We live in societies – what's happening in that society will have an impact on your mood in ways you may not be directly aware of.

Useless emotions

While most emotions are useful, even the heavy or 'bad' emotions like anger, sadness, frustration, and fear, because they galvanise you to act and bring about change, there are three useless emotions that do nothing but trap you and make you inert. These emotions are regret, envy, and worry. They are useless because they don't stimulate you to change your situation; rather, they burn energy while keeping you passive.

Regret keeps you dwelling on the past. Dwelling on the past is like watching a bad film at the cinema – it's already been filmed; you can't change it to make the plot better or the ending happier. Instead, you're just stewing in the dark, thinking what a terrible film it is. That's not taking action; it doesn't change anything or help anyone. There is a much more helpful way to think about the past and deal with any negativity surrounding it.

EXERCISE: REFRAMING REGRET

Good for all personas

Think about things that happened in the past that you regret, perhaps times when you wish you had done something, or that you hadn't, or there was something you wish had gone differently. Write down what you learned and gained from the experience. Even if it is just, 'I will never do that again', that's an important life lesson – but try to go into detail. What warning signs or red flags can you look for to avoid being in that situation again? What aspects about the situation in particular can you identify or isolate that you especially want to avoid?

For example, let's say you had a job at a terrible company and ended up burning out. It doesn't help to think, 'I wish I'd never taken that job' because it's already happened, you can't change that. Instead, spend some time writing about what exactly made that job so bad for you. Was it a manager who wasn't supportive? Were you doing the job of two people after a colleague quit? Did your team expect you to be available twenty-four seven? Thinking about it in detail will help you identify the 'deal breakers' that you will not be willing to put up with again. Armed with this knowledge and attitude, you can actively seek a future work situation that gives you what you want.

Envy is dwelling on others' accomplishments, skills, talents or lives and wishing you had them yourself. We all feel envious sometimes. There's a reason it's one of the seven deadly sins – it's part of the human condition, it's normal. But that doesn't make it good for you.

Everyone is dealt different cards in life. Some people are born into rich families (in America, we call it 'being born on third base' because you're already three-quarters of the way to scoring), happy families, or mentally well-adjusted families. Some people are born in cities, regions or countries where education was good and/or free, where they feel safe and they have access to food and clean water. Some people are born into terrible circumstances, but have good physical and mental health and the energy and strength to try to change their circumstances. Some people start out badly but have help from teachers, caregivers, healthcare or social work professionals, and are able to turn their lives around. Some people are particularly clever, some are particularly attractive, some are particularly lucky.

Comparing your circumstances and path to anyone else's is useless and counterproductive. When you dwell on what other people have and what they are doing, you're not thinking about or doing anything for yourself.

EXERCISE: REFRAMING ENVY

Good for all personas

When you notice feelings of envy toward someone you see on the news, social media, or in your life, try to identify what exactly it is that they have and you don't. Write a list of the specific things you envy and then group them into two categories: the hand they've been dealt, and things you can achieve yourself.

The first category should include anything related to their past and their circumstances: their family background, generational wealth, their upbringing, education, their relationships, good physical or mental health, and so on. There's nothing you can do to make your hand the same as theirs.

The list of things you can achieve yourself could include money, but it can also include personality traits and characteristics you want to develop in yourself. This is especially useful if you're envious of other people's romantic relationships. While you can't force the luck of meeting the right person, you can develop personality traits that will make you a better romantic partner, such as learning how to listen better. It can also help you figure out where to insert and position yourself in life – for example, if you want to be more like successful tech entrepreneurs, you can attend events where people are guided on how to develop their start-up ideas.

You can use this list to set goals for yourself (see the later exercise on goal setting).

Worry is dwelling on the future, usually running projections of negative outcomes of possible actions in the present. It's a natural human emotion, but I know many people (myself included) who can become absolutely paralysed with worry and can't function. It is often associated with anxiety and panic attacks.

Imagining negative outcomes can also be linked to childhood trauma.[62] If you were abused or neglected as a child, especially before the age of five, then it may have felt like bad things happened for seemingly no reason. To try to make sense of chaos, children can imagine reasons and rules as coping mechanisms; these can include magical thinking and catastrophising (or catastrophic thinking).[63]

Magical thinking is things like, 'If I tap this door three times before I go out, my parents will be in a better mood.' This can develop into superstitious behaviour or even OCD in adulthood.[64] Catastrophising is thinking through every scenario that could happen as a result of the current situation, so you can convince yourself that you will be emotionally and mentally prepared for any outcome, even the worst possible outcome. This can turn into paralysing worry, or again OCD, in adulthood.[65]

The exercise below can help you deal with worry in a healthier and more productive way. This exercise can be challenging if you suffer from chronic anxiety and/or panic attacks, so if that is you, please consider doing it together with a therapist. In addition, if you suffer from excessive or paralysing worry, I recommend that you limit or eliminate your access to news. News outlets and social media make money from fear, so they hype up disasters and project worst-case scenarios for situations that may well resolve themselves in less negative ways. It does not help you to ground yourself in the now if you have headlines screaming that the worst is about to happen. If you feel the need to stay up to date, I recommend finding sources of fact-led news with a balanced perspective, not ones capitalising on fear-mongering and clickbait.

EXERCISE: REFRAMING WORRY

Especially good for Survivors and Erasers

When you find yourself worrying excessively about the outcome of a particular action or situation you are in, try the following:

Observe the stories you're telling yourself about those potential negative outcomes. What can you identify as your particular fears? For example, the worry that comes up most often for me when I want to do something 'risky' (taking time out to write a book, for example) is, 'I'm going to run out of money and end up homeless.' This is a persistent worry that causes me to have panic attacks, especially at night.

Then start imagining some possible positive outcomes. These can be realistic, or your wildest dreams. In my example, this could be that the book I write is hugely successful and helps lots of people. But imagine if it became a bestseller; imagine if I'm invited on Oprah to talk about it. Any positive outcome is possible because the future is not set. The idea is to encourage you to see the negative outcome you're fixating on as just one of many possible futures. This increases objectivity and distance.

If your worry is causing you anxiety and stress day to day, ground yourself in the here and now. For example, if I'm worried about running out of money in the future, I remind myself that I have the money I need in the present. Do I have enough to pay my bills and feed myself today? Yes. Do I have enough for the week? Yes. Enough for the month? Yes. Would my friends help me if I ran out of money short term? Yes. Would I end up homeless? Absolutely not. Ground yourself in what is true now.

Another way to ground yourself in the present is to make a gratitude list. That is a list of things you are grateful for today. Try to make it as long as possible and include things you might take for granted, like having access to clean water and food, feeling safe in your home, having weekends and holidays, having access to healthcare. This can help you remember that your life in this moment is good and stop you from focusing on fictional futures where things are bad.

Note that if your worry is a legitimate and real one (for example, if I did *not* have the money I need today), I would call that an issue, not a worry. This exercise is about those negative fictional future scenarios that we extrapolate from our present, things that may never happen.

Procrastination

This is another thing I personally struggle a great deal with. An article in the *Washington Post* had this great line about procrastination: 'For many people, procrastination is a strong and mysterious force that keeps them from completing the most urgent and important tasks in their lives with the same strength as when you try to bring like poles of a magnet together.'[66] Studies suggest that procrastination chronically affects 15–20% of adults,[67] and that around 25% of adults consider procrastination to be a defining personality trait.[68] I suspect that percentage is higher in people with Imposter Syndrome. Researchers and psychologists have identified various causes of procrastination, including perfectionism;[69] fear of failure; fear of criticism; low self-esteem; and a disconnection with the future self and/or future goals (ie understanding how the task will contribute to your life/goals).

Does this sound familiar to you? Given what we've already talked about, you can see why Imposter Syndrome sufferers would be more likely to have problems with procrastination than others. Getting over procrastination is about practising forgiveness. For those of us who beat ourselves up about our perceived flaws, when we procrastinate, we feel guilty about it. Dealing with this guilt only makes the procrastination worse. Instead, you need to forgive yourself. Explicitly say to yourself 'I forgive you.' This is similar to the work we did on regret. You can't change that you procrastinated in the past, it's already happened. Start over by forgiving yourself for your past behaviour and then look forward to the future.

EXERCISE: BEATING PROCRASTINATION

Especially good for Survivors and Differents

I find that I procrastinate when I'm presented with, or present myself with, a huge goal. Again, I'll use the example of writing a book. A whole book, with thousands of words and hundreds of pages – terrifying. The way I've learned to approach writing a book is to set myself a minimum number of words per day, with no editing, just getting the words onto the page. I can edit later. This is how I overcome the terror of the blank page.

You can do the same thing with other tasks and goals. Break it down into the smallest steps possible, and do one step now. Just one. If that step seems impossible, try breaking it into even smaller steps. Make these steps as small as they need to be for you to feel like you can start. If all you can do right now on that big presentation is to start up your laptop and open up the presentation software, and that's it, congratulations, you've taken the first step. Now take a break, reward yourself by putting on a song and having a little dance for a few minutes, then come back and do the next small step. Usually, once you've taken a couple of small steps, you get into a rhythm and can do more for longer.

In the previous SuperEgo Parent exercise, you put some 'I want to' exercises on your to-do list along with the

'I have to' demands. Now try doing a creative 'I want to' task right before the work you need to do. That activates the creativity centre in your brain and makes it more capable of thinking about complex tasks. Once you have finished a step from your list, do another creative, fun thing. It's a reward for your inner child and keeps your brain focused and elastic.

Procrastination is exacerbated by the SuperEgo Parent. When you're driving yourself from 'I have to' to 'I have to', you leave little room for self-determination and creativity. When you have a list of things you *must* do and the presentation for work is given equal weighting as folding the laundry and cleaning the kitchen, you're going to default to the laundry or the kitchen, because it's checking off a 'have to' without having to think or engage your creativity. It's less effort for the same psychological payoff. The exercise above will help you distinguish between different types of activity and get into the right frame of mind for each.

EXERCISE: POWER 15

Another one of my favourite anti-procrastination techniques is the Power 15. If you are *really* struggling to start something, try promising yourself that you will do it for 15 minutes then take a break and do something fun. That could be 15 minutes of work followed by an hour of video games; 15 minutes of work, one episode of your favourite TV show.

> Usually, it's the act of sitting down and starting that is the issue. Once you break the seal of procrastination, you often end up being able to work for longer than that 15 minutes. If it's a struggle though and you can't, honour your promise to yourself and take that fun break, then come back and try another Power 15.

Some final tips on overcoming procrastination: one way to break through fear of criticism or failure is to plan work sessions with people who think you are great. If you're struggling to overcome paralysing fear, ask them to remind you of your accomplishments, or even share with them your thoughts on the thing you're currently struggling with. When I have sat with friends and written, getting immediate positive feedback has helped me.

Also remind yourself what your goals are for this project and how they will contribute to your future success. This doesn't even have to be about your career or some lofty future goal. It helps even to just say to yourself, 'If I get this presentation done now, I can relax and enjoy the concert tonight, instead of worrying.' When you have been successful in achieving a goal that will help you in the future, when that time arrives remember to thank your past self for doing it. This creates a positive neural pathway in your brain between your present, past and future selves.

The external judge

I had a coaching client say to me, 'I feel bad that I am not as far on in my career as I'm supposed to be.' I said, 'Supposed to be? According to whom?' She couldn't answer, other than a vague reference to where friends or colleagues were in their paths. It is common for Imposter Syndrome sufferers to feel that they are failing against externally set criteria, even though they can't articulate who is judging them or what the criteria are exactly.

This is a common problem amongst people who grew up with demanding parents or caregivers and who had a lot of expectations imposed on them in regard to performance at school/college/university, sports and extracurricular activities. At school we do have external judges in the form of teachers and a set of criteria against which we are judged, in the form of exams and assessments. If these are given too much weight in childhood, those children can grow into adults who continue to feel that they are being judged against an externally imposed set of criteria.

You might think that's not necessarily a bad thing. We want to perform well in life and having a standard to meet will help push us to succeed. But where does this standard come from? And what happens if you fail to meet a standard you have set for yourself?

The answer to those two questions will determine whether the external judge is serving you or not. If your criteria, your standards, are set by you, in a positive way and focused on your path, they can be useful. But if you strive to meet unrealistic criteria based on looking with envy at other people's paths and not taking into consideration your own strengths, skills and talents, it will just be a stick to beat yourself with. For example, imagine if someone said 'I should be a rock star' but they couldn't sing or play any instruments. I have heard of examples of criteria that people have set for themselves that are almost as far-fetched as that – and they beat themselves up when they inevitably didn't meet them.

If when you fail to meet a standard you've set for yourself, you say, 'Okay, I've learned that was not an achievable goal, what lessons have I learned?' this can be useful. But people with Imposter Syndrome frequently set themselves impossible criteria and then, when they fail to meet them, see it as proof of how useless they are. This can cause two things to happen: they stop believing in their ability to direct their own lives and/or they lose the ability to proactively set goals and standards for themselves in the future. This adds up to feeling like a victim of life rather than having agency.

When I conducted my survey, 38% of people agreed with the statement 'I don't feel like I've accomplished as much as I'm supposed to by this time in my life', and more than a quarter of respondents strongly agreed. This means that almost two-thirds of respondents perceived some set of criteria that they were failing to meet. This can be extremely demotivating and discouraging, so let's do something about it.

EXERCISE: WHO'S THE JUDGE?

Good for all personas

If you have the sense that you are 'behind' in your life somehow, that you have not accomplished as much as you're supposed to, the first step is to get clarity about what exactly you mean. Write down the things you feel you should have accomplished by now, everything you can think of. Done certain things in your career? Met a partner and started a family? Made a certain amount of money? Bought a house? Run a marathon, written a book, spoken a language, lived in a foreign city? Write it all down.

Then, consider each item on the list and think to yourself, 'Why is this here? Is this something I actually want, or something I'm supposed to want?' For example, if you haven't progressed as much as you were 'supposed to' in your career, who decided what level of progress was acceptable? You? Your parents? Or are you comparing your life to your peers, heroes, or people you've seen on social media?

For the things that you actually want, figure out why you don't have them. This is tough because it can make you feel bad about yourself, but often the reason is not (entirely) you. If you are not where you want to be in your career (note the change from 'should' to 'want' here), why is that? Maybe you started later than your peers because you travelled, took breaks, or initially went down a different career path. Maybe you took time off to have children or take care of sick family members. Or maybe the job you're in is not best suited to your particular skills and talents. If you suspect this to be the case, it's important to note that this is not a failing, it's simply a lesson learned. You can then think about what roles might be better suited to your particular set of skills and talents. Many people change careers at some point in life, and change on one's CV is no longer the red flag it once was. So, don't be afraid to consider a career change.

If you have money on your list, this is especially important to think about. Often, we want money because it means security, freedom, or both. If you feel you do not have enough money, is it because you don't feel secure in your life? Or because you want the freedom to do or have more? Once you have identified what is driving your desire for more money, you can make a plan to help you save for the specific things you want to do or have.

If there are things on your list that you want to accomplish and you can let go of the fact that you haven't yet, you can turn them into future goals. Setting goals is proactive and allows you to own your criteria for success.

8
Your Stories

We all grow up with stories, in books and in fairy tales, as well as stories passed down through families. They teach us the rules we need to function in society. Our brains respond best to information presented in a narrative way.[70]

We have a particular reaction to the stories people tell us about ourselves. We tend to believe them, long after those stories might go out of date, if they were ever true at all. Stories about us tend to be told and retold by our assigned family members: 'Remember that time you peed in the pool?', 'Remember when you were in the school play and forgot all your lines?' These stories connect us to our past, but they can frequently be negative, or remind us of unhappy times.

We carry negative stories with us into adulthood. I carried the story that I was lazy, a story told to me all through my childhood, into my adult life. Turns out, I wasn't lazy, I just struggled with procrastination due to a crippling fear of failure. But until I learned that about myself and updated the story to reflect the truth, the 'Lauren is lazy' narrative played in my head every time I couldn't force myself to do something I needed to. That story was never true, but I needed to actively work on letting it go.

These stories can also be developed in adulthood. Our filters can tell us negative stories about ourselves that we believe, even in the complete absence of evidence. One of my coaching clients asked me to help her with a problem she had identified as 'I can't have difficult conversations with the people I manage.' I already knew her and didn't believe that story to be true, based on what I knew about her. I asked her to give me some examples of when she had struggled with this problem, or when this supposed failing had been mentioned in performance reviews or comments from managers or peers. She could come up with just one example. I said, 'Could it be that you are beating yourself up unnecessarily about this one situation, which may have been beyond your control, because you have an underlying belief that you should be able to handle any situation you face?' Given the fact that she had subsequently had other difficult conversations with other team members, it was fairly obvious that this was a story she was telling herself based on an underlying perfectionism, so we were able to resolve it as an untrue (and unhelpful) story.

EXERCISE: UPDATING YOUR STORIES

Good for all personas

Write a list of the negative stories that you have been told or that you tell about yourself, that you still believe in.

For example:

- I am lazy
- I am not good at X (writing, art, sports, meeting new people, a skill in my job, etc)
- I am too loud, too soft, too shy, too aggressive, too emotional ('too' anything, essentially)
- I cannot do X (anything you believe you can't do)
- I do not deserve X (especially 'I do not deserve to be happy')

For every statement on your list, knowing this is merely a story that may or may not be true, write down what evidence you have for this claim. Has anyone in your adult life ever said this to/about you? Have you tried to do something as an adult and failed?

For example, perhaps as a child you were told by your assigned family you weren't good at sports. Every Christmas, as an adult, they tell the story they remember (or made up) about how you weren't good at sports. As a result, you don't do anything athletic in your adult life. But other than those stories from childhood, what evidence do you have that you're not good at sports? Maybe you're not a professional athlete, but few of us are. What does it mean to you to be 'not good at sports'? Does repeating that story serve you in any way? Maybe it gives you an excuse to get out of group activities with friends, but is that because you actually don't want to participate or because you're scared to look stupid? Does it keep you from having fun with friends or colleagues and being physically healthy? Is it any use to you at all?

Try telling yourself a new story. Instead of, 'I'm not good at sports', you tell yourself 'I haven't found a sport that I enjoy yet.' This gives you the option to try new sports and activities and, if you don't like them, you still haven't yet found the right sport. Keep trying until you find one that you do. How 'good' you are at it doesn't matter.

The goal is to create new stories that don't stop you from trying new things or believing in your ability to do things.

Life is not about only doing the things that you're good at. Life is about trying lots of different things, having different experiences and connecting with people. Believing and continuing to tell negative stories about yourself stops you from trying new things, or from doing things purely because you enjoy them, and not worrying about the end result. They make you a less interesting person, someone who lives a small life. Re-examining those old stories, leaving some behind and choosing to tell yourself new stories can get you out of the trap that's keeping your life small.

Feelings of obligation

Humans are social animals. We are all connected to others and this connection is a healthy, natural thing to want. In the Imposter Syndrome survey I conducted, I asked whether people agreed or disagreed with the following statement: 'I feel obligated to go to social events that I've agreed to attend, whether I'm in the mood or not.' More than 46% of respondents agreed and another 25% strongly agreed. Many Imposter Syndrome sufferers have an extreme sense of obligation when it comes to their relationships with other people. This can be linked to family obligations that are imposed upon us as children by adults who may not understand that children's needs are different to adults', possibly because they themselves were expected to be or do certain things for their family.

This can manifest in a feeling of obligation to those in our chosen family, or our friendship group. If you regularly put the needs of others before your own, this might be due to a misplaced feeling of obligation because you have previously been made to feel that other people's needs are more important.

Obligation can manifest in many ways. You can feel obligated to put up with someone's bad behaviour because you don't want to lose them as a friend. You may feel obligated to take care of a family member even though you don't have the energy to do so. You may feel obligated to stay in a job because you feel loyalty to the company or person that hired you, even though it's now holding you back. It is not always easy to identify when acting out of obligation stops being about maintaining good relationships and becomes damaging to your life, but it's important to make sure you are still taking care of yourself. A metaphor I like to use with my coaching clients is the announcement flight attendants make before take-off: 'If oxygen masks are needed, please make sure to put your own mask on before helping others.' They say this because there are plenty of people in the world, especially parents, who focus on other people first. But if you've passed out from lack of oxygen, how can you help others? You need to prioritise your mental and physical health so that you are strong enough to provide help to others. The next exercise will help.

EXERCISE: UNPICKING OBLIGATIONS

This is particularly good for Erasers

Relationships sometimes place more weight on one person than the other. It's not helpful if you treat it too much like a transaction or equation, where everything I do for you has to be balanced out by something you do for me. But it helps to learn more about those relationships where you feel obligation, to ensure that you are also taking care of yourself in the situation.

Who are the people you feel obligated to? Are they assigned family, chosen family, friends, colleagues? Do you feel obligated to everyone, or are there specific people in your life that you are more willing to help? Are there some people who ask a lot from you? Why do you feel like you need to help them? Are there things you're doing for those people that are stopping you from doing things for yourself? Do you balance helping others with taking care of yourself?

Write down some thoughts in response to the questions above, especially the last one. You may not be able to change the obligations you have to other people, but it is important to understand where these obligations came from, why they exist and what the cost is to you.

Some obligations can feel heavier than others, and many are bound up with complex emotions. An easier place to start is the social events you commit to. Sit down with your diary and categorise your social activities into two lists:

1. Events you're looking forward to
2. Events you're not excited about but feel obligated to go to – include in this list any that you were initially excited about but now aren't

Look at the second list: why do you feel obligated to attend these events? Who else is going? Is it assigned family, chosen family, friends? Can you identify the feelings that come up when you think about not going? Are you afraid of what other people might think? Are you worried that those people will no longer like you? Do you have FOMO (fear of missing out) and think that if you don't go, you will be out of the loop or seen as uncool? Be honest with yourself about why you feel obligated to go.

Next, divide the obligation list into three categories:

1. Genuine obligations, events you cannot miss – a wedding, a family birthday party, something

significant in the lives of your family/friends that won't be repeated
2. Events you could miss but are worried about upsetting someone or looking bad
3. 'FOMO' events

For events that fall into the second category, try turning them down but suggesting an alternative plan. I hate big parties and feel bad when friends have big 'ragers' for their birthday because I just don't want to go. When I decline the invitation, I suggest a different event, like taking them out to lunch, instead. This makes them feel special and appreciated without my having to attend a big party where I will feel uncomfortable.

There is a particularly crap section of the second category, which is work events you're 'expected' to go to. Know that you cannot be required to attend work events outside of work hours. Can it be awkward to not go to them? Yes, especially if you have managers or colleagues who judge employees by the wrong criteria. I will not pretend that these types of events don't lead to some employees being preferred over others. If you know that your manager or colleagues are these types of people, I would suggest you approach this as you would a work goal, not a genuine social event. Go, if you know it's the way to get ahead, but have goals for when you're there (eg talk to and be seen by the people who need to know you're there), don't drink too much and go home once people stop keeping score. In other words, treat these events like networking events.

Finally, don't be surprised if a number of your social obligations fall into the FOMO category. This phenomenon is a particular challenge for people suffering from Imposter Syndrome, as FOMO 'was found to be associated with a lower sense of having one's needs met as well as a lower feeling of life satisfaction in general'.[71] If you feel FOMO about an event, try going and noticing your feelings while you're there. Do you feel more 'in the know' or like you're at the centre of things? I bet you don't, because FOMO is based on the erroneous belief that other people are living better lives than you are, a belief exacerbated by social media.

A positive note on FOMO – it tends to disappear as we get older. Lived experience on the one hand, and decreasing energy on the other, together convince us that it's unlikely that any event is going to be so amazing that our life will be considerably enriched by it. In my middle age, I have real JOMO (joy of missing out). I'm not concerned that anything better is happening elsewhere.

Sharing your feelings

Another distressingly common symptom of Imposter Syndrome is the feeling that you can't or shouldn't burden other people, even those close to you, with your problems. This is a tough one to unpack, because it frequently reveals a belief, taught in childhood, that your problems are not important; that if you tell other people your problems, they will like you less, or even leave you.

When I asked my survey respondents whether they agreed or disagreed with the statement, 'I don't like to burden other people with my problems', a whopping 85% either agreed or strongly agreed. Nobody enjoys having problems and wants to share those with others, but there is an underlying belief in some people that to share problems is to place a burden on others. The disinclination to burden other people with problems is one of the few symptoms of Imposter Syndrome that I think affects men and women equally, perhaps men even more. Men are taught and socialised to not talk about their pain, fears or worries with other people, except perhaps their significant other.[72] Men also don't go to therapy as much, or for as long, as women, as it is still not as socially accepted for men.[73] It is unsurprising then that men commit suicide at on average three times the rate of women and also struggle much more with addiction issues.[74]

EXERCISE: SHARING

Good for all personas

Make a list of the people you share your problems with. How long is the list? Many people, men especially, have just one person they feel comfortable sharing their problems with. But what if that person isn't available, either literally or emotionally, because they're dealing with their own problems?

It's important to create an emergency contact list of at least three to five people with whom you can share deep emotions or feelings with. If this is a struggle, think about people in your life who are sympathetic, who may have shared things about themselves with you in the past, are good listeners and/or have had similar issues as you in the past.

Then, have a conversation with the people on your list, to test the waters, so to speak. You can use this exercise as an excuse to start the conversation: 'I'm reading a book that says people should share more with others, what do you think about that? Do you share your feelings with other people?' See how they react. If they are interested, if they agree, if they confirm that they do share feelings with other people and think it's important, they are a good candidate for your list. If they seem uncomfortable with the idea or don't want to talk about it, they're probably not.

But if they seem open, start deepening the conversation by asking them about an issue they have had in the past. Sometimes it's less confronting to speak about something you know is resolved, as they may feel more comfortable talking about it. For example, you could say, 'I know you and your wife were having trouble a couple of years ago, but things seem better now. How did you work on getting past that?' This would also give you the opportunity to broach the subject if you were having trouble in your own relationship, if you wanted to.

The above exercise may seem basic to some people, but research has shown that it is difficult for adults to make new friends, or deepen the friendships we already have, because this kind of bonding is related to shared experience, which we have less of as adults. That's why so many people find new friends in work colleagues. It also means that a good way to meet potential new friends is to pursue group hobbies or participate in regular meetups related to things you're interested in.[75]

It can't be overstated how important it is to have a few close friends with whom you discuss your feelings and fears, not just one person upon whom you depend for everything. Loneliness amongst adults is so bad it has been described as an epidemic, which has only been made worse by the Covid-19 pandemic in recent years. Loneliness is literally bad for you – research has shown that loneliness is associated with early mortality, depression, anxiety, heart disease, substance abuse and domestic abuse.[76] So invest the time and effort into deepening the friendships you have and seeking new connections. It might save your life – and theirs.

9
Your Filters And Triggers

This chapter will focus on how we understand and filter the information and input we receive from others. Few people think about what they say to others, or how they say it. People are not often taught how to communicate in optimal ways. They also generally have quite a lot of noise in their heads and negative thoughts, and don't have the space or time to consider how their words will land with the other person. Or perhaps they don't care, or are in pain and want to inflict pain on others. You also may not be hearing others' words as they are actually meant, because of filters and triggers that come from within you. Filters and triggers are among the greatest challenges that Imposter Syndrome sufferers face, and are therefore the things they benefit most from overcoming.

Your filters

We filter all the information that we receive. We do this completely unconsciously and, in a lot of cases, these filters are helpful. Say you meet someone and while talking to them, you start to feel as if they aren't trustworthy; your gut instinct is telling you that their body language is not matching their words. Many behaviourists and psychologists say we can 'read' people unconsciously and tell when they're not being honest, with themselves or others.[77/78]

But many of us also have filters that do not serve us. If you suffer from body dysmorphia and, for example feel that you are fat when you're not, and someone tells you, 'You look great in that outfit', your filter might make you think they're lying to you or just trying to be nice, when in fact they probably mean exactly what they're saying. You are literally unable to process and understand the words they're saying because of your filters. As with triggers, becoming aware of the filters you instinctively apply can reduce their effect. Unlike triggers, though, you can actually get rid of some of your filters, and they do change throughout our lives (some for the better, some for the worse).

As a result of internalised fears and negative beliefs about yourself, you are incapable of truly listening to what other people are saying. You are unable to process and understand the words they're saying because of your filters. Becoming aware of the filters that you are applying to your interactions with people is almost impossible to do by yourself, you need other people. There are various techniques you can use for this type of exercise; I give you my preferred method in the exercise below.

EXERCISE: IDENTIFYING YOUR FILTERS

Good for all personas

In doing this exercise, you will need to work with one or two other people, who should be fans of yours. Ask them to write a list of at least ten things they like about you, including personality, emotional, physical (eg 'I love your eyes') and relationship traits.

They should then read the list to you, slowly, one by one. The first time through, just listen to what they say and pay attention to your reactions. Check your feelings about each item on the list. What makes you feel uncomfortable and where in your body do you feel the discomfort? Do you find yourself thinking, 'That's not true' or 'They're just saying that to be nice'? Note down your reactions.

Ask them to read the list again, and after every item on the list, say 'Thank you.' That's it, just 'Thank you'. If you feel the urge to say anything else, a disclaimer or a deflection ('Oh but your eyes are nicer'), write it down instead.

Once you're done, take a look at what you've written down. Were there particular things on their lists that you had strong reactions to? Think about the stories you have attached to those things.

For example, someone might have said, 'I like your fashion sense.' You might have a bad reaction to that because your mother did not like what you wore when you were a teenager and told you that you dressed badly (according to her taste). You may not be able to hear these kinds of compliments as an adult, because you have a filter running that says, 'I have bad taste in clothes.' You have programmed your brain to hear those compliments as insincere or a lie. Once you identify the old story that has created that filter, you can update it as we practised previously. Update it with a new story that says 'I have my own style in the way I dress and I like it.' Try listening to those compliments again with this new filter.

It's important to do this work with people who love and support you, as you want their positive input. Filters are often linked to quite negative, often hurtful stories and so this exercise might bring up some heavy emotions. I find this to be particularly true with older stories, or stories about our physical bodies. If you try this exercise and find that it upsets you, it's a good idea to work with a therapist to discuss the emotions, memories and insights that come up.

Your triggers

In recent years, people have mocked the idea of triggers, claiming that people are too sensitive. I don't believe people are any more sensitive than they have been in the past; the difference is that people finally feel they have the space to talk about how negative language – including racist, homophobic or sexist comments – makes them feel. In general, this is a good thing, as we are becoming more aware of the powerful, historical, cultural, and deeply personal effects of language.

Everyone has particular subjects or language that trigger them, because we have all had negative experiences that we associate with certain words or concepts. If you grew up with a parent who told you that you were 'being stupid', you will likely have a negative reaction if someone comments, 'Oh, that was stupid' about something you do, even if it is clear they are joking. Your reaction may be disproportionate to the situation in the present because you are being triggered into responding as that child did in the past. Emotional memories are extremely powerful, especially negative ones. When you are triggered, you can be plunged into an emotional memory that you feel just as intensely as if you were still in that moment in childhood.

It helps to become aware of the words, concepts and things that trigger you because it is unconscious and instantaneous, so will likely happen for the rest of your life. By becoming aware of your triggers, you can lessen the intensity and duration of the triggered feeling, so that you feel better faster. I know this is possible because I have done it. I used to be triggered by many things, but I have lessened the impact of the triggered feelings by becoming aware of how and when I'm being triggered and what in my past it's connected to.

Triggers are like switches in your brain that are connected to past emotions and experiences. If you find yourself becoming disproportionately angry or upset at something someone does or says to you, it is most likely triggering painful memories and emotions from the past. The word 'disproportionate' is key here. What I mean by that is a reaction that exceeds what is warranted or might be expected in the actual circumstances. If someone does something to deliberately injure you and you become upset, that is a proportionate, or appropriate, reaction. But if your reaction is bigger and longer lasting than is appropriate in the context of what is actually happening, for example if someone has (clearly) accidentally hurt or upset you and you react as though it were deliberate, you are most likely being triggered by something in the past rather than the present.

I can give you an example from my life. In a previous relationship, I was living with my boyfriend and one day I hadn't taken the clean dishes out of the dishwasher and put the dirty ones in. When he came home, he said in an irritated voice, 'Why don't you ever do the dishwasher?' I became insanely angry and did not speak to him for three whole days. He was irritated and maybe he didn't handle it in the best way, using the words 'why don't you ever' which was untrue, as I had in fact unloaded the dishwasher on occasion. But did this warrant the level of anger that I felt (and expressed)? Did he deserve to not be spoken to for three days? No, definitely not.

After a lot of work with a therapist, I tapped into childhood memories of being told I was a slob who never cleaned. This created a trigger for me that meant I became very upset when someone implied (they didn't even have to actually say it) that I was not a good housekeeper, especially someone I loved. Once I became aware of my trigger, I could catch myself before I reacted and say to my boyfriend, 'I need to go and cool off, I'm being triggered by this.' I could spend time by myself 'rightsizing' the situation in the present.

'Rightsizing' is not about pushing the problem away, ignoring it, or assuming you are in the wrong. It means looking at which parts of what you're feeling are true and relevant to the current situation (in my case, my boyfriend had expressed himself carelessly – he was in a bad mood, so he overstated the problem) and which parts are related to the trigger and are not relevant to the given situation (he didn't say I was a bad housekeeper, or call me a slob). Then you can return to the situation or discussion able to admit your mistakes ('You're right, I should empty the dishwasher more often, I will work on that') and react proportionately to what has upset you ('Could you try to express yourself better'). The exercise below will help you get to grips with rightsizing as a way to tackle your triggers and keep your reactions proportionate.

It's worth bearing in mind that this topic, like filters, is another hard one that again can bring up a lot of difficult childhood or past memories and so again, if the exercise below brings up particularly difficult feelings or upsetting memories, consider working with a therapist to explore these safely.

EXERCISE: IDENTIFYING YOUR TRIGGERS

Especially good for Survivors

Pay attention to when you may be having a disproportionate reaction to events and situations in the present. A good indicator of this is an anger spike. Examples might be when someone criticises your work, you feel angry even though it wasn't meant to be personal. Or when someone implies that a remark you've made wasn't thought through – you feel like they're calling you stupid and immediately get upset. Or when someone thoughtlessly cuts you up in traffic and you become furious.

If you are having an extreme reaction in the present moment, try to get away from the situation as fast as possible, without reacting too much. While you're being triggered, it is basically impossible to be rational because your reaction will be coming from the part of your brain that is feeling panic, fear and stress, the part that thinks you're in a life-or-death scenario. You can't have a rational discussion in a burning building. You may not be able to stop yourself reacting – that's okay, it happens. You can apologise once you've calmed down.

When you've calmed down enough to be able to analyse your reaction, write down the details of the event. Focus especially on what happened right before you began to react disproportionately. Who was speaking? What were they saying or doing? What kind of language were they using? You want to try and figure out what the trigger was. If you can, write it down alongside the way it made you feel. In the example I gave earlier, I would write down, 'He said "Why don't you ever do the dishwasher" and I heard "Why are you such a bad housekeeper? Why are you such a slob?"'

The next step is tricky, but try to work out *why* that trigger made you feel the way it did. Does it relate to a childhood feeling or experience? Write down some ideas. It may take some time and practice to uncover these things, this isn't easy work.

Once you know how this person or event made you feel, and maybe why it made you feel that way and what that's connected to, you can start 'rightsizing' it. Think about what *actually* happened and what part the other person played. Was what they said unfair? Worded badly? Spoken in anger or expressed in a hurtful or insulting way? Write it down, using 'I' statements as much as possible: 'I felt that because he used absolute language, he was being unfair in his statement and taking out his irritation on me.'

Then think about your part in it. Did you do or say something wrong? Write down what you could do differently, using only future tense. Do not beat yourself up for past mistakes, because remember that film has already been made, you can't change what happened. Write down what you could do or say differently in the future if the situation occurred again.

When you're calm enough, you can go back to the person who triggered you. You can start by explaining your reaction and why you needed to leave the situation before you could resolve it. This is also a good time to apologise for anything hurtful you said while triggered – explain that you were reacting from a place of extreme emotion that was unrelated to what was happening in the present.

Then present the situation as you saw it – their part and yours. Apologise for anything you did wrong and make a commitment to work on those things in the future. It can help to use your actual notes from this exercise, especially the first few times you try it, as you get used to this way of communicating. You are training your brain to think and express itself in a new way, so it can be helpful to follow a structure initially. Eventually, you may not have to write anything down at all and can do it all in your head.

A final note on triggers: Know that triggers that stem from childhood, or particularly painful triggers, might never go away completely. I compare it to a knot in a tree: when a tree is wounded, it can't heal the wound the way animals can. Instead, it grows layers on top and bulges out in what's called a 'burl'. A deep wound in our psyche might not ever fully heal, even after years of work. But what we can do, by becoming aware of and working through our triggers and response, is to lessen both the depth and the duration of our reaction to a trigger.

With practice, it can get much easier to become aware in the moment that you're being triggered and to do

YOUR FILTERS AND TRIGGERS

the work of 'rightsizing' then and there, especially if you explain your triggers to those close to you. Then, when it happens, they understand what's happening for you in that moment. Remember, triggers are not your fault, they're not of your choosing, so it shouldn't be shameful to admit them to those who love you. Most of us have them too and will understand.

PART THREE
TAKING UP SPACE AND EXERCISING AGENCY

Here comes the fun part. Some of the exercises in part two can be quite difficult and heavy. This next batch of exercises may not be easy, but they are focused on helping you take an active step toward a future where you suffer less, or not at all, from Imposter Syndrome. A future where you take up space and exercise more agency. Many sources of Imposter Syndrome are there to convince us to take up less space and be smaller in the world. Every instinct you have to be smaller (physically, through dieting and taking up less physical space, or figuratively, by keeping quiet in meetings or groups) or to apologise for your existence and use of oxygen comes from external pressures to not embody your physical power.

I don't want to focus excessively on the role of the patriarchy in all this, but it is directly responsible for the internalisation of the feeling that we are not allowed to take up the space that we are entitled to. Since it is so pervasive amongst people in general, though especially non-white and non-male people, there must be a common societal cause. I argue it comes from a scarcity mindset, a belief that there is not enough for everyone.

I've already spoken at length about the cost of allowing people to limit themselves. The exercises in this third part of the book are designed to help you take the space and agency you deserve. No more, no less. They're not designed to make you a loud, toxically cheerful person who sucks up all the oxygen and energy in the room with their relentlessly positive attitude. They're designed to make you a more present, stronger version of you, exactly as you should be.

'Taking up space' means defining and reinforcing your boundaries. I've talked already about people who have grown up being told or shown that they should erase themselves to make room for others, whether that's because those others are ill, narcissistic, or not empathetic. Taking up space means reasserting your mental, emotional, spiritual and physical space, the space that belongs to you as a human being who is just as valid and worthy as any other.

I like to use the metaphor of the bag on the seat. You know when you get on a crowded train, all the seats are taken and someone has their bag on the seat next to them. Are you the type of person who asks them to move their bag, or do you stand there silently seething? If you're the person who seethes, then you have internalised the belief that you don't have the right to claim that space. You're not alone in this, of course. Just look around at all the other people standing and seething. But expecting the person whose bag is on the seat to suddenly become more empathetic is a waste of your energy. Try politely asking them to move the bag. They might refuse, they might seem annoyed, or they might apologise. Their reaction is their business. What's important is that you stood up for your right to claim that space.

Enabling you to 'exercise more agency' is the second aim of these exercises. This first requires an understanding of what agency is. Having agency means having – and perceiving – control over your actions and their consequences. This is important for people with Imposter Syndrome, as they can frequently feel that they have little to no control over their actions and/or what happens to them in life. Have you ever thought that you don't make good decisions, or that you don't make decisions at all? A number of my clients have said things like, 'Stuff just happens to me; I don't feel like I consciously decide to go one way or the other.' These people discount the role of their intuition in helping them make decisions, because they believe that decision-making requires logical, conscious thinking. They also don't analyse their mistakes, or choices that have led them in the wrong direction, to try and learn from those choices, because in their minds making mistakes is always wrong. The reframing regret exercise earlier in this book will help you learn how to turn mistakes into learning opportunities, and the external judge exercise will help you to stop judging yourself so harshly for perceived mistakes. But in this section, we're going to focus on how to make more conscious and directed decisions to build agency and use it to defeat Imposter Syndrome. When you believe in your ability to make good decisions, you are more capable of actioning goals, taking risks and trying new things.

10
Dreams And Goals

Everyone has dreams. Dreams about the way we're going to live start when we are very young. Ask any child what they want to be when they grow up and you will see their dreaming in action. When I was five, I was positive that I would be a ballet dancer. Every child has those dreams, even if what they grow up to be ends up being quite different.

At some point in our journey of growing up, we are taught to be 'more realistic' about our dreams. For some, that's helpful. For example, if you dream of being a professional footballer but you aren't any good at football, it's okay if that dream is tempered by a dose of reality at some point in your childhood and teen years. But for those who grew up with some or a lot of the conditions that breed Imposter Syndrome, that gentle 'tempering' can be more like dream crushing. Hillary Clinton has often told the story of how she wrote to NASA when she was thirteen, asking how she could become an astronaut, and someone wrote back saying that women can't be astronauts.[79] This was sixty years ago and women can be, and are, astronauts now, but many children's dreams are still being crushed in this way by people who think they're being helpful.

If you suffer from Imposter Syndrome, the dreams you have in adulthood are probably (too) small and (too) achievable. For example, 'make enough money to live comfortably', 'have a family', or 'get a job where I can use my degree'. I would argue these are not dreams at all, merely life events. You will probably achieve those 'dreams' pretty quickly and easily and then wonder what you're supposed to do with the rest of your life. When I ask people with Imposter Syndrome what dreams they have for the rest of their life, they often can't articulate anything at all. Dreams require a certain amount of belief in oneself that they don't have.

How do you develop bigger dreams? Take a look at your goals. 'A goal is a dream with a deadline.'[80] Goals are easier to access for many people than dreams, since dreaming big seems scary. The exercise below will help.

EXERCISE: GOAL DOUBLING

Good for all personas

Write a list of at least five goals. Any kind of goal, professional or personal, big or small. The only exception is any kind of diet or weight-loss goal, which we do not want to use for the purposes of this exercise.

Then try doubling those goals. This might involve making a goal more detailed, shortening the timeline to achieve it, any way that feels bigger than the original. Make them more concrete, more impactful, more long-lasting. Double them again and again, until they look impossible, scary and not like anything you could achieve. 'Get a job in the field in which I got my degree' might increase to 'Become a leading authority in my field', which could become 'Be regularly invited to speak on my area of expertise', which could develop into 'Actively look for three speaking opportunities in the next year'.

Once you've done this for all your goals, select one of those bigger ones to take action on. Write a plan for how you could make it happen. Taking the 'Actively look for three speaking opportunities in the next year' example, who do you know who speaks at conferences in your industry? One of the action points in your plan could be to contact that person and ask them how they get invited to speak at conferences. (If you are nervous about contacting that person, the making connections exercise later on will help.) Research conferences in your industry that relate to your area of expertise. Write an outline of what you could talk about at an event, discuss it with colleagues and see what they think. They might have some insight into conferences or events where you could speak. If you have a fear of public speaking, you're not alone – it is estimated that around 75% of all adults are afraid of public speaking.[81] Sign yourself up for a course or workshop to build your confidence in public speaking.

None of these actions are committing you to actual speaking opportunities. You can explore every aspect of a goal in detail to ensure it's something you want to pursue before committing to it. If you decide that it's too much work, or too scary, for right now, you can change your mind. No one is grading you on your life choices, so try anything and everything on for size to see what fits. But if you can, try not to let fear discourage you from seeing some of these things through, because the payoff for setting yourself a Big Hairy Audacious Goal and then achieving it, is unlike anything else in the world.

And you *are* capable of it. The part of you that says you aren't is just telling you old stories that can be left behind.

11
Finding Your People

For some reason, people don't seem to spend a lot of time telling each other how awesome and amazing they are. It is odd that is not 'the done thing' to tell the people you're close to what they mean to you. I tell my loved ones all the time just how wonderful I think they are, and why. Even the ones who are uncomfortable with it (mainly my English friends) accept it and respond in kind. I'm a big believer in being an active fan of other people.

Activate your fan base

You have fans, even if you don't know it. You may think you're moving quietly through life, unnoticed and unappreciated, but that is your Imposter

Syndrome lying to you. I guarantee there are people who think you are fantastic. Do you have friends? A romantic partner? Colleagues who hang out with you even when they're not required to? Family members you stay in contact with? If you do, then you have fans. No one has the time or energy to hang out with people they don't like.

It will help you hugely in overcoming Imposter Syndrome if you can identify and activate that fan base for yourself. When other people believe in you and tell you how great you are, it can counteract at least some degree of self-doubt. Especially if you've done the filters exercises above and can truly hear and understand what they're saying without dismissing it. Use the exercise below to identify your fan base.

EXERCISE: FINDING YOUR FAN BASE

Especially good for Survivors and Erasers

Make a list of all the people with whom you have positive relationships; positive meaning they seek out your company and you seek out theirs, you have interesting conversations with them, they make you laugh and make you think, and vice versa. You share hobbies or interests. You have warm feelings toward them and look forward to the next time you will see or speak to them.

When you have your list, ask each of these people why they like you. I know, this is so awkward and embarrassing. Do it anyway. Be honest and tell them it's for this exercise. If it's too uncomfortable for either of you, ask them in a text or email and give them some time to think.

The list that you receive may be what I will call a 'qualified list'. This is a list of your positive characteristics with that person's judgements attached. For example, someone might say, 'You are really clever, but you don't rub it in people's faces.' The second part of this statement says more about what their experiences with 'clever' people in the past have been like than it does about you, so you can disregard it.

There may be overlaps in the lists you receive from each person, but you should hopefully end up with up to ten unique things that people like about you.

Now rephrase the items on the list to make them all 'I' statements: 'You are really clever' becomes 'I am very clever', etc.

Now take your list and stand in front of a mirror at a distance where you can see your face clearly and read the list out loud to yourself. Do this at least once a day, preferably several times, for at least two weeks. You will probably feel silly at first, but keep doing it. Pay attention to which statements are most uncomfortable for you to say. Which statements feel untrue? Keep practising saying these things to yourself for at least two weeks.

For any statements that feel untrue, try to think of specific evidence that would prove them to be true. Using the above example, you would try to recall moments or times when you felt you were demonstrably 'very clever'. If you can't come up with any examples, go back to the person who said it and ask them why they think it. They will probably be able to give you several examples.

If some things are particularly hard to believe, even with evidence, think about why you don't believe them. Perhaps you grew up in an academically accomplished family, but you did not succeed in a traditional school setting, so perceived everyone around you growing up to be smarter than you. But the adult you has had opportunities to learn and gather experience in non-academic ways, including self-study, work experience, or mentoring. Challenge your definition of what 'very clever' looks like. It doesn't have to be about getting top grades and high test scores, it could be about having the ability to execute, to compete, to perform, to problem solve.

Choosing your family

Earlier in the book I drew a distinction between your assigned family and your chosen family. Your assigned family is the people you grew up surrounded by, whether it's birth parents and siblings, adopted parents and siblings, foster families or other caregivers. People you didn't choose to have in your life but were, for a significant period. Some of these people might have been great influences and some might have been terrible. Whatever they were for you, you had no choice in the matter, you were simply born into, or found yourself in, the situation.

It's unclear where the term 'chosen family' originated, but it might have come from the roots of slavery in countries like the United States where many slaves were torn from their birth families and uprooted from their homes. They created new families in their new circumstances, developing significant relationships with those around them.[82] This practice has also been adopted by LGBT+ youths who have been forced out of or rejected by their assigned families because of their sexual orientation or gender expression. The TV show *Pose* depicts 'houses' where older LGBT+ people take in young adults who cannot remain in their family homes and would have otherwise ended up homeless. They adopt traditional roles such as 'House Mother' and 'House Father' and those who go to live there are loved and supported as if they were their biological children.

As an adult, you can choose who you call your family, no matter what your childhood situation was. Not every adult is good at parenting. Many parents do not know how to show, tell or teach children that they are loved and that the things they care about matter. Additionally, assigned siblings may not provide love and support during childhood and adolescence. This may be because they are not close in age, or because the parents do not encourage or reward sibling relationships, or for other reasons.

I had a mentor who described a chosen family in adulthood as a 'prosthetic family' – people who complete you, who give you the support and love you may not have received in from your assigned family in childhood, like a prosthetic taking the place of a missing limb. You can have good relationships with your assigned family and still have a chosen family in adulthood. The exercise below will help you to identify your chosen family and recognise their influence on your life.

EXERCISE: CHOOSING YOUR FAMILY

Good for all personas

Make a list of the people outside your assigned family who have helped you throughout your life. These can include teachers, mentors, coaches, therapists, friends, managers, colleagues, etc. Generally speaking, this shouldn't include people with whom you've had a romantic relationship, as that is a relationship of a different kind.

Next to each person's name, summarise how they have helped you. Did they encourage you in a certain area of study? Did they help you identify and understand your emotional triggers? Did they show you that you were worth a lot to them by helping you through a difficult time in your life? Did they help you to feel more competent in a job?

Who on that list is still in your life? Are they still supporting you in that way, or has your relationship changed? If the people on that list are no longer in your life, do you still have people who are supporting you emotionally and helping you learn (excluding any romantic partner)? If the answer is no, use the sharing exercise from earlier to try and increase the number of people in your life who can provide emotional support.

It is important that you have a couple of people in your life who are older (either literally or in terms of emotional maturity) who can provide at least occasional advice and support. An elder, a mentor, a coach, whatever you want to call it. We continue to need a form of parenting through our entire lives; without people who can support you and provide wisdom, you can end up feeling very alone. If your own parents can function in those roles, you're very lucky. Even if that's the case, having mentors in your chosen field is still advisable, as your parents are unlikely to be able to help you with career decisions.

If doing the above exercise made you realise that there are people in your life who play the role of your chosen family, you might want to share this with them – it may be exactly what they need to hear from you.

Making connections

If you don't have them already, how do you find people to provide mentorship, advice or insight into your chosen or future career? A common thing I see amongst people with Imposter Syndrome is a fear of contacting older, more senior people in their industry, or even anyone outside their immediate network. This seems to stem from a belief that they would be wasting those people's time. It's also commonly tied up with a fear of rejection, which I will address later, since it's such a big topic. Even for people who are willing to risk rejection, many of them don't know where to start. The exercises below will help you explore ways to expand your contact list and make new connections.

EXERCISE: FINDING CONNECTIONS

Good for all personas

The easiest way to look for people to connect with is online. In a professional context, the most reliable tool is LinkedIn, as the majority of people in business have a profile there and are actively looking for connections on that platform. You can also see what mutual connections you already have and can then ask your contacts' advice on how best to get in touch with interesting people.

Helpful things to consider when looking for new contacts are, do they have a job or a career that seems interesting to you? This could be something further along the same career trajectory as you, or maybe in a new direction you're thinking of exploring. Do they speak at events, organise interesting meetups, live in a location you want to find out more about, or do interesting volunteer work? Also look for people who are sharing thought-provoking content.

Another way to explore potential new contacts is to talk to friends, colleagues and existing contacts about the type of people you're interested in meeting. For example, if you're thinking about changing careers and would like to find out more about innovation work, you could ask friends if they know anyone working in innovation. People are generally predisposed to be helpful and if you give them a clear indication of specifically what you're looking for, they will help if they can.

A third way, which is mostly geared towards extroverts or people who prefer to connect in person, is to attend networking events on the topic or in the industry you're interested in. If you don't like networking events and/or find it awkward to make small talk, you can work on improving your networking ability.[83] Some good tips are to prepare some icebreakers, such as 'What are you passionate about?' and bring someone with you so you don't get stuck in the corner on your own while you work up the nerve to speak to people.

The most important thing with the above activities is to be clear on your 'ask'. What do you want from the people you hope to connect with? If it's more information on what a job in a certain industry is like, or how to get started in that career direction, be clear about that. If someone has moved from your country to Singapore and you want to know what that experience was like, ask them specifically about that. Being specific helps people to help you. It also shows people who don't know you that you're not wasting their time. A specific request in an initial contact is much more likely to receive a response than a general 'get to know you' contact.

But what if you're not looking for specific information? What if you do just want to get to know someone because you'd like a mentor, or because you think they seem cool and interesting, or you want more contacts in a particular industry? Then it's important to do your research so that you're not simply 'cold calling' a stranger.

EXERCISE: REACHING OUT

With the ubiquitous nature of the internet, it's easy to learn a lot about a person from a simple Google search. If you want to connect with someone, look them up first. What articles, blog posts, or opinion pieces have they written? Are they sharing videos on YouTube or TikTok? Do they have a website, either personal or professional? Read what they have to say and look at their posts on Instagram, Twitter or Facebook, wherever it is that they 'hang out' digitally.

When you contact that person, reference something of theirs that you've engaged with and that sparked your interest. Compliment them on their interesting take, their well-researched opinion, or their clever video and tell them why you liked it. It's a good icebreaker, as it starts a conversation about something you may have in common.

It's a good idea to stick to professional rather than personal topics on channels generally understood to be for business purposes (ie LinkedIn or if you've made contact through a business website). Keep compliments either professional or friendly, nothing that could be construed as relating to physical appearance. A good rule of thumb is, would you pay this compliment to a relative? If not, don't send it to a stranger.

You could send a link to an article (from a reputable source) you've found interesting on a topic they have written or spoken about before, with a comment like, 'Given your expertise in this area, I wondered what you thought of this recent article on X in *The Guardian* yesterday?'

If they respond, remember to clearly articulate your ask. I recommend asking them for a short call or chat over coffee sometime in the next couple of weeks. For a first meeting, always propose no more than half an hour and respect that person's time – be punctual and don't take up any more of their time than you have requested. Once that time is up, acknowledge it and propose a next step, if relevant. If the person has time to keep talking, let that be their choice.

Prepare a few questions before you meet. This is easy if it's about a specific topic, but even if it's just a general 'get to know you' session, it's good to have a few things to talk about that show you've done your research. Focus on them to start with, no matter what your ultimate goal is. They are sharing their limited time, so show that you appreciate that.

A good way to close any initial conversation, especially one where you've received information, is by asking, 'Is there anything I can help you with?' This does two things immediately: it makes it clear that you understand that they've given you something, and it also makes the relationship reciprocal, potentially extending its longevity as the person will more likely to want to interact with and help you again.

Simply put, making connections helps you achieve your goals. Expanding your network can make more things possible and provide access to advice, learnings and resources you wouldn't otherwise have. It is crucial for Imposter Syndrome sufferers to understand that the only thing holding them back from making connections is fear – fear of rejection or of burdening other people with their needs. But we all need help and if you ask respectfully, patiently and with good reasons, people are generally willing to provide it.

Understanding and dealing with rejection

I touched already on people's fear of rejection. There is a good physiological reason for this. Rejection registers in the brain similarly to physical pain and the reaction is the same to both.[84] Research has shown that once we associate a certain behaviour as having the potential to inflict pain on us, we will actively avoid it – avoidance of potential future pain is a major driver of human behaviour.[85] In the context of Imposter Syndrome, this means that if you think you're likely to be rejected because of, or while, performing a certain activity, your brain will try to prevent you from doing it. It will come up with a tidy, logical explanation: 'It's no use doing that again, it won't work.' This is just fear, which is your brain trying to protect you from something it thinks might hurt. It can be even worse for people who suffer from chronic depression or anxiety, as the corresponding pleasure response when something they feared turns out to be successful is so muted that there is no motivation to even try.

Knowing what's happening neurologically is helpful when you're trying to do something that scares you and you're feeling a lot of resistance. It's not you being a scaredy-cat, or lazy, or anything like that. You are just trapped in a rejection-avoidant cycle that your brain is perpetuating.

EXERCISE: THREE TIMES RULE

If a person you reach out to doesn't respond, don't take this personally – they don't know you, how could it be personal? Your email or message might have come on a particularly busy day. I advise you use the 'three times' rule. Send one follow-up message a week or so later, giving that person the benefit of the doubt (I typically use a line like, 'I'm sure your inbox is jammed right now and I wanted to climb to the top of the pile again'). Then one more, a couple of weeks later. If there is no response after three messages, move on with your life. It isn't personal, you did your best, but you have no idea what they have going on – they simply may not have the time or energy to communicate with a stranger.

There is no easy way to overcome fear of rejection, but I will give you a few tips that I've identified over my many years of having not just fear of rejection, but Rejection Sensitive Dysphoria, a condition frequently associated with ADD/ADHD.[86] This advice centres on how you understand the word 'no', in a professional and networking context.

- 'No' is not personal and it's not your fault. When a person turns you down, it's almost always about them. They may not be capable of providing what you're asking of them (not your fault). They may not have the head space, understanding, time, resources, or mental clarity to give you what you need (not your fault). Even if they say it's about you, it's not – it's based on their understanding or perception of you, which you cannot control. It can also be about timing, luck, the weather – any number of things you cannot influence and are not your fault.
- 'No' is an opening bid in a negotiation. I find there are cultural differences here – Europeans are much more likely to say no to an opener than Americans, for example. If they are responding to you at all, even if it's a no, this begins a dialogue that you can continue. If someone says no, you could ask, 'Can you tell me what the gap is between it being a no and it being a yes?' Just try it once. You may not get an answer, but you won't lose anything and if you can continue the dialogue and get past the no, it will sometimes end up with a yes.
- 'No' feels like shit and it's okay to let it get you down. If you've done all the right things and it's something you really wanted or needed, but you

get a no, it feels like shit. Let yourself feel it, then remind yourself of all the reasons why it isn't about you.

- 'No' can be an opportunity to learn. If you feel like you can and dare to ask for feedback, do it. Often, people are afraid of feedback because they think it's going to make them feel bad about themselves. Feedback is actually valuable insight. When someone takes the time to give you feedback, they are giving you insight into how to get what you want next time. Pay attention, this is valuable information.

If you can get beyond your fear of rejection and try a few times to contact people, apply for jobs, whatever it is you're trying to do or access, an interesting thing often happens – you get better at handling rejection. Think of it like exposure therapy. Your brain learns, through repeated exposure to the terrifying thing, that it actually isn't that scary after all. Rejection won't kill you, even if it hurts.

When you do get rejected, I recommend that you write down any feelings that come up. This will help you process those feelings and get past them, potentially avoiding them in the future. Keep those notes for the future – they will be a helpful reminder that rejection, and the feelings it sparks, won't kill you. The next time you need to put yourself out there and are afraid of being rejected, it will help to remind yourself that you've survived it once already and can again.

Decision-making

Many Imposter Syndrome sufferers think that they are bad at making decisions, or that they make bad decisions. Introverts and Erasers in particular may believe that they take too long or dither too much over decisions. But decision-making can be challenging for anybody who struggles with feeling regret, worries too much about what other people think about them, or compares their life and progress to other people or where they think they 'should' be.

You will make many decisions in your life, big and small, and not all of them will be good ones. But no decision is final. It you fuck up, you can always unfuck yourself. You can almost always save a bad decision, even if takes a lot of effort. As long as you're alive, you can change your life. If you are someone who often feels regret, or feels it particularly strongly, the reframing regret exercise from earlier in the book is a good one to work on, as regret reinforces a belief that you are bad at making decisions.

EXERCISE: DECISION-MAKING

Good for Introverts and Erasers in particular

When you are preparing to make a big decision, always use that tried-and-true tool – the pros and cons list. Try to make it as detailed and comprehensive as possible. Make a list for every option, including the option of doing nothing at all.

In situations where you don't have all the information, make an additional list of the knowns and the unknowns for each option. If you can shorten your list of unknowns with additional research, do so. This list might tell you what questions you need to ask in the case of applying for a new job, for example.

When you have the pros/cons and the knowns/unknowns for all of the options, rank them in order of priority, as not all pros and cons will carry equal weight.

Ordering your options based on priority will make your choice feel logical and fact-based, rather than random and intuitive. But you should account for your intuitive feelings about the different options, giving it an actual weight alongside facts. If you think 'that job looks the best on paper, but that hiring manager wasn't willing to introduce me to peers I'd be working with, and that felt weird', write it down.

When you have made a fact-based decision and it turns out to be a mistake, it will probably be because of the unknowns. Something not working out because it was an unknown cannot be your fault.

It can also mean that your priorities are different to what you thought they were when making the decision. That means you've learned something about yourself and can make better decisions in the future. It's not a mistake if you have learned something from it, no matter how it may feel in the moment.

For example, say you are looking for a new job. You find two that you're interested in and you apply. You have a good feeling about both, but one pays more and the other is more convenient, with flexible working conditions and hours. You make pros and cons lists for four options:

1. Staying in your current role
2. Continuing to look for other opportunities
3. Job one that pays more
4. Job two that offers more flexible working

You use what you've learned about both jobs from your discussions with company representatives, from research you've done and conversations with people in your network.

When ranking the options, you prioritise making more money over flexibility because you're saving up to buy a house. Given all you know, what you've researched and the analysis you've done of the different options and your priorities, you choose the job that pays more.

Flash forward six months and you realise you've made a mistake. Yes, the job pays well but they expect you to work all hours and respond to emails night and day. You might be able to afford a house faster, but you'd never be home to enjoy it. Your impulse might be to kick yourself and regret the decision you made, but there were things you didn't know about the situation and things you've learned about yourself that are helpful. Now you know that quality of life and flexible working conditions are more important to you than a high salary, even if it takes you a longer time to reach your goal of buying a house. You can now look for a new job knowing more about what to prioritise and what questions to ask a prospective employer.

12
Loving Yourself

The idea of loving yourself might make you cringe – trust me, I understand. It also may seem impossible for anyone who lacks strong self-belief and struggles to acknowledge their own strengths, talents and skills. But, like everything I recommend in this book, it *is* achievable. It can help to approach it scientifically, so let's talk about love and what exactly it is.

Love is a chemical process that triggers the production of dopamine, oxytocin and serotonin, the so-called 'happy hormones', in the brain.[87] A lot of the brain lights up when we produce dopamine. It also can trigger the stress hormones, cortisol and adrenaline, which is why we get butterflies in our stomach and can even feel physically ill in the presence of a crush.

Even modern science cannot help us understand why we fall in love with some people rather than others. There are theories that it's to do with smell, that we can literally smell when someone is genetically and chemically compatible with us and develop an attraction accordingly. What we call 'love at first sight' may in fact be 'love at first smell'.[88]

While falling in love seems to be chemical, staying in love requires something different. It requires a mutual respect and appreciation, as well as continuing communication.[89] Common advice on keeping the love alive in a relationship includes:

- Continuing to take care of and support the other person
- Listening to them and taking their desires and problems seriously
- Forgiving them when they make mistakes
- Avoiding being overcritical, insulting, or overly harsh, even when arguing

All of the above should also apply to your relationship with yourself. Yet people who suffer from Imposter Syndrome have been trained, socialised or told to not to support themselves, not to listen to themselves, not to take their needs seriously, not to forgive themselves and to be hypercritical of themselves when they make mistakes.

As an Imposter Syndrome sufferer, how do you learn to fall – and stay – in love with yourself? If you've managed to do any of the exercises in this book, you've already taken the first step. All of the exercises are designed to help you become aware of your behaviours, even those you don't like or that contribute to your Imposter Syndrome. In learning about your (often unconscious) behaviours you can identify which are true reflections of who you are and who you want to be, and which are the result of programming by other people and do not serve you.

When you become aware of who you truly are, who you choose to be, you have a much better chance of loving yourself. Even if you discover parts of yourself you don't like, you can increase your love for yourself by finding them. None of us is perfect and we don't expect it of others. Our flaws only enhance our positive characteristics.

To love yourself, you need to listen to yourself and take your needs seriously. If you are not allowing yourself a certain amount of pointless fun per week (which can include doing absolutely nothing), you are not taking your needs seriously. Working out, eating healthy food, doing 'worthwhile' things are fantastic for your health, but may not fulfil your inner child's need to play, dream and imagine.

You also need to consciously forgive yourself. Don't push away feelings of shame, guilt or embarrassment if you make a mistake. Talk it through with yourself the way you would with a partner or close friend. Acknowledge what you did wrong and 'rightsize' what actually happened. Was the mistake really that bad? What was the actual impact on you or others? Is it as devastating as it feels right now, or are you having a disproportionate reaction because you've been triggered? Then, identify what you learned from the experience. Even if the only lesson is that you're not going to do something again, it's still a lesson learned.

Finally, never use hateful, hurtful or insulting language when talking to yourself; talk to yourself as you would your partner or close friend. Hurt people hurt others. When turned on yourself, this creates an even more vicious cycle. Remember, if you make a mistake or a wrong decision, a lesson can always be learned. Speak lovingly to yourself.

EXERCISE: LOVE LETTER TO YOURSELF

Good for all personas

This might be the most difficult, but also the most rewarding, exercise in the whole book. I want you to write a love letter to yourself. If you've ever written a love letter to someone, whether you sent it or not, you'll know that it is focused on what makes that person special to you, for what they do and for who they are. Even if you've never written one, you will likely have thought about what you love in someone else.

I guarantee that you can come up with at least five things you love about yourself. If you're stuck, look back at the list of things other people have said they admire in you.

Can you think of moments you were kind? Brave? Honest, when a lie would have been easier? Made a good decision? Made someone laugh? Picked out the perfect gift? Helped a friend in need? Managed a project well? Put together the perfect outfit? Smiled at someone just because you felt happy? It doesn't matter if something was only momentary, as long as it made you feel good about yourself. These small moments are what life is made up of.

Finally, add to the list anything you love about your physical body. Even if you suffer from body dysmorphia, I bet there are things you like about your appearance. Your eyes, your smile, any tattoos, your choice in clothes, how you do your makeup – any aspect of your appearance. If you can see past the negative filters that hide the truth, you can appreciate your amazing self.

Now you have all the ingredients of a love letter to yourself. Ideally, write the letter by hand and make it as long as you can. It might go something like this:

'Dear Me, I love that you are so kind and caring towards other people. I can tell it makes you happy to make them laugh and smile. I think you're smart and you have creative thoughts and ideas. I know you are working on being brave and telling the truth in confrontational situations. I am so proud of the work you've done on that and I saw when you disagreed with your manager last week. That was so brave. You also have such beautiful eyes. I love your aesthetic and that your clothes express your creative and artistic spirit. I just love you.'

Who wouldn't want to receive a letter like that?

Write love letters to yourself every week. Treat this as a way of reflecting on all the positive things you were, did, felt and learned from that week.

If you like drawing, you could illustrate the letters with images that spark a positive memory or remind you of one of your favourite things about yourself. Use coloured pens. Write the letters on beautiful stationery and keep them in a special box. Treasure them as you would letters from a lover and read through them periodically to remind yourself of all the wonderful things you've been and done over time.

Conclusion

Imposter Syndrome is insidious, affecting more of us than we know, and it's so damaging. When I started my coaching work, I was extremely disheartened by the number of people who seemed to be suffering, alone and in silence, from the same things. Over and over, I would hear, 'I can't do that', 'I'm not good enough', 'I'm too afraid to try something different', 'What if I fail?', 'Other people are better than me', 'I can't do normal things', 'I don't want to burden other people with my problems'. Everyone has those kinds of thoughts from time to time, but a devastating number of us feel them so often, so intensely, that they are miserable, trapped in a small, unsatisfying life.

My aim for this book was to try and help more than the otherwise few people I might be able to personally connect with in my lifetime. I want this book to help stimulate a public conversation about Imposter Syndrome, its societal and personal causes, and its costs. My dream is for people to be less afraid to say out loud, 'I don't know how to handle this' and to ask for help. Change first requires de-stigmatisation, permission to talk about it and ask for help.

The exercises in this book are not easy to do and they require commitment and effort. Some of them may bring up difficult feelings, thoughts and memories. But if you bought this book, you probably have a strong motivation to put in the work. Admitting you are suffering and need help is a huge step.

Remember you are not alone in feeling the feelings that may come up. Talk to people about your journey. Ask for help. Look for support groups – there are many out there, a lot of them are free or only ask for a small donation (such as twelve-step groups, which are worldwide). Get professional help if it's available to and/or affordable for you. You deserve the help, and you deserve to feel better.

My purpose with this book, and with the workshops I give, and all of the videos, podcasts and other content I produce, is to create a safe space and initiate a public dialogue about Imposter Syndrome. I would love you to share with me your experiences dealing with Imposter Syndrome and your feedback on this

CONCLUSION

book. This is a condition that gets better with sunlight – as we talk about it, the burden gets lighter and things get better for subsequent generations. Remember that sharing helps us all to feel less alone. None of us needs to be alone and feeling like an imposter any longer.

References

1 'How to ask for a raise and get it', Payscale (no date), www.payscale.com/research-and-insights/how-to-ask-for-a-raise, accessed 3 August 2022
2 H Marks, 'Stress symptoms', WebMD (19 August 2021), www.webmd.com/balance/stress-management/stress-symptoms-effects_of-stress-on-the-body, accessed 10 August 2022
3 F Devi et al, 'The prevalence of childhood trauma in psychiatric outpatients', *Annals of General Psychiatry*, 18/15 (2019), https://annals-general-psychiatry.biomedcentral.com/articles/10.1186/s12991-019-0239-1, accessed 31 July 2022

4   K Springer et al, 'The long-term health outcomes of childhood abuse', *Journal of General Internal Medicine*, 18/10 (2003), 864–870, www.ncbi.nlm.nih.gov/pmc/articles/PMC1494926, accessed 31 July 2022

5   H Markus and P Nurius, 'Self-understanding and self-regulation in middle childhood', *Development During Middle Childhood* (National Academies Press, 1984), www.ncbi.nlm.nih.gov/books/NBK216782, accessed 31 July 2022

6   B Amsel, 'The effects of parental involvement on self-confidence and self-esteem', GoodTherapy Blog (16 July 2013), www.goodtherapy.org/blog/effects-of-parental-involvement-on-self-confidence-and-self-esteem-0716134, accessed 31 July 2022

7   C Adams, 'The effects of self-centered parenting on children', *Psychology Today* (13 May 2022), www.psychologytoday.com/us/blog/living-automatic/202205/the-effects-self-centered-parenting-children, accessed 3 August 2022

8   K Rigby, 'Consequences of bullying in schools', *The Canadian Journal of Psychiatry*, 48/9 (2003), 583–590, https://doi.org/10.1177/070674370304800904

9   C Higgins, 'The age of patriarchy: How an unfashionable idea became a rallying cry for feminism today', *The Guardian* (22 June 2018), www.theguardian.com/news/2018/jun/22/the-age-of-patriarchy-how-an-unfashionable-idea-became-a-rallying-cry-for-feminism-today, accessed 10 August 2022

10 JC Williams, 'The 5 biases pushing women out of STEM', *Harvard Business Review* (24 March 2015), https://hbr.org/2015/03/the-5-biases-pushing-women-out-of-stem, accessed 31 July 2022

11 B Günel, *We hebben al een vrouw ('We already have a woman')* (Mediawerf, 2017)

12 'Think again: Men and women share cognitive skills', American Psychological Association (2014), www.apa.org/topics/neuropsychology/men-women-cognitive-skills, accessed 10 August 2022

13 H Devlin, 'Use of male mice skews drug research against women, study finds', *The Guardian* (31 May 2019), www.theguardian.com/science/2019/may/31/sexist-research-means-drugs-more-tailored-to-men-says-scientist, accessed 10 August 2022

14 N Hodgins, 'How long Covid is shaping up to be a feminist fight', Refinery29 (10 March 2022), www.refinery29.com/en-au/long-covid-impact-on-women, accessed 10 August 2022

15 L Kiesel, 'Women and pain: Disparities in experience and treatment', Harvard Health Blog (9 October 2017), www.health.harvard.edu/blog/women-and-pain-disparities-in-experience-and-treatment-2017100912562, accessed 31 July 2022

16 M Galmiche et al, 'Prevalence of eating disorders over the 2000–2018 period: A systematic literature review', *The American Journal of Clinical Nutrition*, 109/5 (2019), 1402–1413, https://doi.org/10.1093/ajcn/nqy342

17 N Kumar, 'Eating disorders in men are not talked about enough – and they're on the rise', Healthline (23 November 2021), www.healthline.com/health/eating-disorders/eating-disorders-in-men, accessed 10 August 2022
18 A Bardone-Cone et al, 'Aspects of self and eating disorder recovery: What does the sense of self look like when an individual recovers from an eating disorder', *Journal of Social and Clinical Psychology*, 29/7 (2010), https://bit.ly/3PfEyno, accessed 10 August 2022
19 R Haskell, 'Bella from the heart: On health struggles, happiness and everything in between', *Vogue* (April 2022), www.vogue.com/article/bella-hadid-cover-april-2022, accessed 3 August 2022
20 W Snipes (@wesleysnipes) 'Don't let the internet rush you...' (14 August 2018), https://twitter.com/wesleysnipes/status/1029435162017259520?lang=en, accessed 10 August 2022
21 M Richtel, '"It's life or death": The mental health crisis among U.S. teens', *New York Times* (23 April 2022), www.nytimes.com/2022/04/23/health/mental-health-crisis-teens.html?referringSource=articleShare, accessed 10 August 2022
22 T Porter, '"Phones are like a scab we know we shouldn't pick": The truth about social media and anxiety', *The Guardian* (22 May 2022), www.theguardian.com/lifeandstyle/2022/may/22/phones-are-like-a-scab-we-know-we-shouldnt-pick-the-truth-about-social-media-and-anxiety, accessed 10 August 2022

23 W Lazonick, 'Profits without prosperity', *Harvard Business Review* (September 2014), https://hbr.org/2014/09/profits-without-prosperity, accessed 31 July 2022

24 K Bhui et al, 'Perceptions of work stress causes and effective interventions in employees working in public, private and non-governmental organisations: A qualitative study', *BJPsych Bulletin*, 40/6 (2016), 318–325, www.ncbi.nlm.nih.gov/pmc/articles/PMC5353523, accessed 2 August 2022

25 J Kelly, 'Indeed study shows that worker burnout is at frighteningly high levels: Here is what you need to do now', *Forbes* (5 April 2021), www.forbes.com/sites/jackkelly/2021/04/05/indeed-study-shows-that-worker-burnout-is-at-frighteningly-high-levels-here-is-what-you-need-to-do-now/?sh=4fefd4c923bb, accessed 10 August 2022

26 J Fuller and W Kerr, 'The great resignation didn't start with the pandemic', *Harvard Business Review* (23 March 2022), https://hbr.org/2022/03/the-great-resignation-didnt-start-with-the-pandemic, accessed 3 August 2022

27 M Perna, 'Toxic work culture is the #1 factor driving people to resign', *Forbes* (1 June 2022), www.forbes.com/sites/markcperna/2022/06/01/toxic-work-culture-is-the-1-factor-driving-people-to-resign/?sh=3d2f0c8068f1, accessed 10 August 2022

28 D Jamieson, 'Amazon spent $4.3 Million on anti-union consultants last year', *Huffington Post* (31 March 2022), www.huffpost.com/entry/amazon-anti-union-consultants_n_62449258e4b0742dfa5a74fb, accessed 10 August 2022

29 N Bowlin, '"Pure propaganda": Inside Starbucks' anti-union tactics', *The Guardian* (4 May 2022), www.theguardian.com/business/2022/may/04/starbucks-anti-union-tactics, accessed 10 August 2022

30 K Morgan, '"Degree inflation": How the four-year degree became required', BBC (28 January 2021), www.bbc.com/worklife/article/20210126-degree-inflation-how-the-four-year-degree-became-required, accessed 10 August 2022

31 TS Mohr, 'Why women don't apply for jobs unless they're 100% qualified', *Harvard Business Review*, https://hbr.org/2014/08/why-women-dont-apply-for-jobs-unless-theyre-100-qualified, accessed 31 July 2022

32 R LeDonne, '"I had impostor syndrome": Taylor Swift talks becoming a director', *The Guardian* (12 June 2022), www.theguardian.com/music/2022/jun/12/taylor-swift-tribeca-film-festival, accessed 31 July 2022

33 MC Perna, 'How skills-first hiring will win out over more traditional hiring models', *Forbes* (10 May 2022), www.forbes.com/sites/markcperna/2022/05/10/how-skills-first-hiring-will-win-out-over-more-traditional-

hiring-models/?sh=276beebd798c, accessed 3 August 2022

34 S Cain, *Quiet: The power of introverts in a world that can't stop talking* (Penguin, 2013)

35 N Doyle, 'Neurodiversity at work: A biopsychosocial model and the impact on working adults', *British Medical Bulletin*, 135/1 (2020), 108–125, www.ncbi.nlm.nih.gov/pmc/articles/PMC7732033, accessed 10 August 2022

36 J Montvelisky, 'Neurodiversity as a strengthening point for your team and our society', *Forbes* (13 August 2021), www.forbes.com/sites/forbestechcouncil/2021/08/13/neurodiversity-as-a-strengthening-point-for-your-team-and-our-society/?sh=21a55f6f28f9, accessed 31 July 2022

37 A Hermanson and M Fares, 'Neurodivergence, war and social justice', Tiimo Blog (3 June 2021), www.tiimoapp.com/blog/neurodivergence-war-social-justice, accessed 31 July 2022

38 RD Austin and GP Pisano, 'Neurodiversity as a competitive advantage', *Harvard Business Review* (May–June 2017), https://hbr.org/2017/05/neurodiversity-as-a-competitive-advantage, accessed 31 July 2022

39 K Strauss, 'More evidence that company diversity leads to better profits', *Forbes* (25 January 2018), www.forbes.com/sites/karstenstrauss/2018/01/25/more-evidence-that-company-diversity-leads-to-better-profits, accessed 31 July 2022

40 M Alexander, '5 ways diversity and inclusion help teams perform better', *CIO* (3 September 2021), www.cio.com/article/189194/5-ways-diversity-and-inclusion-help-teams-perform-better.html, accessed 3 August 2022

41 PJ Zak, 'The neuroscience of trust', *Harvard Business Review* (January–February 2017), https://hbr.org/2017/01/the-neuroscience-of-trust?utm_medium=social&utm_campaign=hbr&utm_source=LinkedIn&tpcc=orgsocial_edit, accessed 3 August 2022

42 E Garton, 'Employee burnout is a problem with the company, not the person', *Harvard Business Review* (6 April 2017), https://hbr.org/2017/04/employee-burnout-is-a-problem-with-the-company-not-the-person, accessed 3 August 2022

43 Survey conducted in May–June 2022 via an online survey with eighty-five anonymous respondents, cited questions were:
'How often have you become burnt out or ill from taking on too much, because you feel like you have to?'
'How often have you hated your job but were unable to even think about what else you could be doing with your career?'

44 R Bastian, 'Why imposter syndrome hits underrepresented identities harder, and how employers can help', *Forbes* (26 November 2019), www.forbes.com/sites/rebekahbastian/2019/11/26/why-imposter-syndrome-hits-underrepresented

-identities-harder-and-how-employers-can-help/?sh=90709ff33c1c, accessed 31 July 2022
45 SA Hewlett, M Marshall and L Sherbin, 'Does a lack of diversity among business leaders hinder innovation?', *The Guardian* (1 October 2013), www.theguardian.com/sustainable-business/lack-diversity-business-leaders-limit-innovation, accessed 3 August 2022
46 Survey conducted in May–June 2022 with eighty-five respondents cited at Endnote 43
47 B Van der Kolk, 'The body keeps the score: Memory and the evolving psychobiology of posttraumatic stress', *Harvard Review of Psychiatry*, 1/5 (1994), 253–65, https://pubmed.ncbi.nlm.nih.gov/9384857, accessed 3 August 2022
48 'Stress effects on the body', American Psychological Association (1 November 2018), www.apa.org/topics/stress/body, accessed 3 August 2022
49 'Cortisol', Cleveland Clinic (last reviewed 10 December 2021), https://my.clevelandclinic.org/health/articles/22187-cortisol, accessed 3 August 2022
50 D Page, 'When cursing is good for your health', NBC News (4 February 2018), www.nbcnews.com/better/health/when-cursing-good-your-health-ncna843776, accessed 3 August 2022
51 'Understanding the stress response', Harvard Health Publishing (6 July 2020), www.health.harvard.edu/staying-healthy/understanding-the-stress-response, accessed 3 August 2022

52 'Prevent pain from computer use', Harvard Health Publishing (1 October 2012), www.health.harvard.edu/pain/prevent-pain-from-computer-use, accessed 3 August 2022

53 C Stieg, 'Working from home during Covid is causing more back and neck pain – here's how to find relief', CNBC.com (3 March 2021), www.cnbc.com/2021/03/03/back-and-neck-pain-working-from-home-amid-covid-exercises-for-relief.html, accessed 3 August 2022

54 Stimming can be defined as 'self-stimulating behaviours, usually involving repetitive movements or sounds'. Source: 'Stimming: Causes and management', Healthline (last reviewed 27 June 2019), www.healthline.com/health/autism/stimming#behaviors, accessed 3 August 2022

55 MK Scullin et al, 'The effects of bedtime writing on difficulty falling asleep: A polysomnographic study comparing to-do lists and completed activity lists', *Journal of Experimental Psychology: General*, 147/1 (2018), 139–146, https://doi.org/10.1037/xge0000374

56 J Crace, '"I feel totally seen": John Crace on how guided breathing soothed a lifetime of anxiety', *The Guardian* (23 May 2022), www.theguardian.com/lifeandstyle/2022/may/23/i-feel-totally-seen-john-crace-on-how-guided-breathing-soothed-a-lifetime-of-anxiety, accessed 3 August 2022

REFERENCES

57 C Miserandino, 'The Spoon Theory', Butyoudontlooksick.com (no date), https://butyoudontlooksick.com/articles/written-by-christine/the-spoon-theory, accessed 3 August 2022

58 Jim Heath Channel, 'James Earl Jones – This is CNN' (2022), www.youtube.com/watch?v=QYJ3d5LTxy4, accessed 3 August 2022

59 K Reilly, 'Why "Nevertheless, she persisted" is the theme for this year's women's history month', *Time* (1 March 2018), https://time.com/5175901/elizabeth-warren-nevertheless-she-persisted-meaning, accessed 3 August 2022

60 V Williams, 'Maxine Waters inspires a new anthem: "Reclaiming my time"', *The Washington Post* (1 August 2017), www.washingtonpost.com/news/post-nation/wp/2017/08/01/maxine-waters-inspires-a-new-anthem-reclaiming-my-time, accessed 3 August 2022

61 'Greta Thunberg to world leaders: "How dare you – you have stolen my dreams and my childhood"', *The Guardian* (23 September 2019), www.theguardian.com/environment/video/2019/sep/23/greta-thunberg-to-world-leaders-how-dare-you-you-have-stolen-my-dreams-and-my-childhood-video, accessed 3 August 2022

62 N Kascakova et al, 'Unholy trinity: Childhood trauma, adulthood anxiety, and long-term pain', *International Journal of Environmental Research and Public Health*, 17/2 (2020), 414, www.ncbi.nlm.nih.gov/pmc/articles/PMC7013389, accessed 3 August 2022

63   M Hutson, 'Magical thinking', *Psychology Today* (1 March 2008), www.psychologytoday.com/intl/articles/200803/magical-thinking, accessed 3 August 2022

64   C Mathews, N Kaur and MB Stein, 'Childhood trauma and obsessive-compulsive symptoms', *Depress Anxiety*, 25/9 (2008), 742–51, https://pubmed.ncbi.nlm.nih.gov/17557315, accessed 3 August 2022

65   R Breazeale, 'Catastrophic thinking', *Psychology Today* (25 March 2011), www.psychologytoday.com/us/blog/in-the-face-adversity/201103/catastrophic-thinking, accessed 3 August 2022

66   A Swanson, 'The real reasons you procrastinate — and how to stop', *Washington Post* (27 April 2016), https://wapo.st/3Qlg3Xg, accessed 10 August 2022

67   P Steel, 'The nature of procrastination: A meta-analytic and theoretical review of quintessential self-regulatory failure', *Psychological Bulletin*, 133/1 (2007), 65–94, https://doi.org/10.1037/0033-2909.133.1.65

68   B Nguyen, P Steel and JR Ferrari, 'Procrastination's impact in the workplace and the workplace's impact on procrastination', *International Journal of Selection and Assessment*, 21/4 (2013), 388–399, https://doi.org/10.1111/ijsa.12048

69   Ibid

70   PJ Zak, 'Why your brain loves good storytelling', *Harvard Business Review* (28 October 2014), https://hbr.org/2014/10/why-your-brain-

REFERENCES

loves-good-storytelling, accessed 3 August 2022

71 E Scott, 'How to deal with FOMO in your life', Very Well Mind (25 April 2021), www.verywellmind.com/how-to-cope-with-fomo-4174664, accessed 3 August 2022

72 M Hamlett, 'Men have no friends and women bear the burden', *Harper's Bazaar* (2 May 2019), www.harpersbazaar.com/culture/features/a27259689/toxic-masculinity-male-friendships-emotional-labor-men-rely-on-women, accessed 3 August 2022

73 P Eil, 'Here's why it's still really hard to get men to go to therapy', *Vice* (22 November 2017), www.vice.com/en/article/43nzag/men-dont-go-therapy-mental-health, accessed 3 August 2022

74 Ibid

75 A Sedghi, 'Loneliness isn't inevitable – a guide to making new friends as an adult', *The Guardian* (30 April 2018), www.theguardian.com/lifeandstyle/2018/apr/30/how-to-make-new-friends-adult-lonely-leap-of-faith, accessed 3 August 2022

76 R Weissbourd et al, 'Loneliness in America: How the pandemic has deepened an epidemic of loneliness and what we can do about it', Harvard Graduate School of Education (February 2021), https://mcc.gse.harvard.edu/reports/loneliness-in-america, accessed 10 August 2022

77 SM McCrea, 'Intuition, insight, and the right hemisphere: Emergence of higher sociocognitive functions', *Psychology Research and Behavior Management*, 3 (2010), 1–39, www.ncbi.nlm.nih.gov/pmc/articles/PMC3218761, accessed 3 August 2022

78 C Raypole, 'Gut feelings are real, but should you really "trust your gut"?', Healthline (no date), www.healthline.com/health/mental-health/trust-your-gut, accessed 3 August 2022

79 M Lee, 'Hillary Clinton's oft-told story that NASA rejected her childhood dream of becoming an astronaut', *The Washington Post* (30 November 2015), www.washingtonpost.com/news/fact-checker/wp/2015/11/30/hillary-clintons-often-told-story-that-nasa-rejected-her-childhood-dream-of-becoming-a-female-astronaut, accessed 3 August 2022

80 N Hill, *Think and Grow Rich* (Chump Change, 1937)

81 R Black, 'Glossophobia (fear of public speaking): Are you glossophic?', Psycom (31 May 2018), www.psycom.net/glossophobia-fear-of-public-speaking, accessed 3 August 2022

82 G Kassel, 'What 'chosen family' means – and how to build your own', Healthline (9 June 2021), www.healthline.com/health/relationships/chosen-family#origin, accessed 4 August 2022

83 A Croft, '6 IRL networking tips for introverts' Firsthand (4 June 2021), https://firsthand.co/

REFERENCES

blogs/workplace-issues/6-networking-tips-for-introverts, accessed 3 August 2022

84 NF Roberts, 'Rejection and physical pain are the same to your brain', *Forbes* (25 December 2015), www.forbes.com/sites/nicolefisher/2015/12/25/rejection-and-physical-pain-are-the-same-to-your-brain/?sh=34f1605c4f87, accessed 10 August 2022

85 C Bergland, 'The neuroscience of seeking pleasure and avoiding pain', *Psychology Today* (1 January 2020) www.psychologytoday.com/us/blog/the-athletes-way/202001/the-neuroscience-seeking-pleasure-and-avoiding-pain, accessed 3 August 2022

86 V Higuera, 'What is rejection sensitive dysphoria?', Healthline (19 November 2021), www.healthline.com/health/mental-health/rejection-sensitive-dysphoria, accessed 3 August 2022

87 'Love is a chemical reaction, scientists find', PBS News Hour (13 February 2009), www.pbs.org/newshour/science/science-jan-june09-love_02-13, accessed 3 August 2022

88 FB Furlow, 'The smell of love', *Psychology Today* (1 March 1996), www.psychologytoday.com/sg/articles/199603/the-smell-love, accessed 3 August 2022

89 R Huseyin, '7 ways to stay in love', Art of Wellbeing (3 August 2018), www.artofwellbeing.com/2018/08/03/stayinlove, accessed 3 August 2022

Further Resources

Many people have written at length about the concepts I discuss in this book and if you're interested in learning more, below are some of the resources I have learned from.

Amen, DG, *Healing ADD Revised Edition: The breakthrough program that allows you to see and heal the 7 types of ADD* (Berkley, 2013)

Brown, NW, *Children of the Self-Absorbed: A grown-up's guide to getting over narcissistic parents* (New Harbinger, 2020)

Cain, S, *Quiet Power: Growing up as an introvert in a world that can't stop talking* (Penguin, 2016)

Clance, PR, *The Impostor Phenomenon: When success makes you feel like a fake* (Bantam Doubleday Dell Publishing Group, 1986)

Fanon, F, *Black Skin, White Masks* (Grove Press / Atlantic Monthly Press, 2008)

Gibson, L C, *Adult Children of Emotionally Immature Parents: How to heal from distant, rejecting or self-involved parents* (New Harbinger, 2015)

Gilligan, C, *In a Different Voice: Psychological theory and women's development* (Harvard University Press, 2016)

Günel, B, *We hebben al een vrouw: Leiderschap en diversiteit in het Nederlandse bedrijfsleven: voorbeelden & valuilen* (Mediawerf, 2017)

Katie, B, *I Need Your Love – Is That True? How to stop seeking love, approval, and appreciation and start finding them instead* (Random House Audio, 2005)

Miller, JB and Stiver, IP, *The Healing Connection: How women form relationships in therapy and in life* (Beacon Press, 1997)

Ruppert, F, *Splits in the Soul* (Green Balloon Publishing, 2011)

FURTHER RESOURCES

Siegel, DJ, *Mindsight: The new science of personal transformation* (Brilliance Audio, 2009)

I also recommend the *Harvard Business Review*; I find that they are consistently creating the best content on psychological issues in the workplace.

Acknowledgements

It is hard to list all the people who have helped me arrive at a finished book about Imposter Syndrome without writing a whole other book. The expression may be that 'It takes a village' but for me, it's been a small city of people who have helped me become an expert and feel confident in my own abilities.

Thank you to Rethink Press, for the top-notch assistance in publishing this book, especially to Sarah Marchant, Anke Ueberberg, and editors Abi Willford and Helen Lanz, who not only helped shape this into a real book, but also put up with the many emotional meltdowns of a first-time author. Thank you to Jane Dixon-Smith for designing the amazing cover, which exceeded my expectations. Also, thank you to Joe

Gregory, who was as passionate as I was about finding the exact right title.

I have had several crucial mentors and guides in my life, all of whom have given me more than I can ever repay. Karen Gaughan and Gil Dove taught me so much about how to be a thinking, caring human. Melissa Marijnen came along at just the right time and reminded me of what I'm worth. Janet Bumpas, Chris Baylis, Andreea Moga, Eve Logunova-Parker and Julia Hart were amazing connectors and generously shared their networks.

Thanks to my beta readers, Julia Hart, Sarah Darweesh and Isabella Mulder, whose enthusiastic response to the draft made me believe even more in this book. Thanks also to my clients, who I won't name, but who know who they are. The exercises in this book were beta tested with them and are rock solid because of it. I also want to thank everyone who responded to and shared the survey.

A special shoutout goes to the team at Rocycle. It is not an exaggeration to say that a lot of this book was conceived while I was riding a bike in class. Thanks to Tiela, Amina, Jeff, Babette, Adina, Joey, Saskia and the whole crew.

Much of the book was written while listening to jazz, especially the amazing cool jazz stylings of Vera

ACKNOWLEDGEMENTS

Marijt, an incredibly gifted pianist who I happen to be lucky enough to know. Get to know her music now – she's about to be world famous.

Thank you to my assigned family. My parents gave me a keen mind, good critical-thinking skills, a strong feminist set of values, and a passionate love of books and learning that led to my being able to write this book. My brother and I learned together that a difficult sibling relationship can be improved in adulthood with communication and caring.

I have an amazing chosen family and it is because of them that I have survived some difficult times in the last few years, so thank you to my friends, including Gérard, Vera, Ben, Isabella, Bob, Jorien, Nikita, Marta, Tadeja, Hayley and the Pathfinder crew. In particular, my ride or die, my bestie, Sarah, who is always, without exception, at the other end of the phone when I need her and makes me laugh harder than I knew I could. I wish for everyone a friend like her.

Also, my fur sons, Tai and Charlie, who keep me alive every day, which is fortunate since they do nothing around the house. They are my ridiculous angels.

And finally, my partner and other best friend, Olly, without whose support none of this would have happened. He always believes in me, even when I can't believe in myself.

The Author

Lauren's career spans three decades. She is a person who has 'reinvented herself' several times. She has founded her own company twice, been a global marketing communications senior professional in tech for many years, developed innovation training and coaching programmes for corporate clients, and has been working with start-ups and scale-ups since the nineties. Her company, Training 2.0, helps people raise their game in their professional and personal lives, through leadership and communication training, as well as executive coaching. She is also a seasoned event host, panel moderator, webinar facilitator, and workshop leader.

Her personal passion is helping people fulfil their potential by transcending limiting beliefs, such as Imposter Syndrome. She is also working to increase the representation of marginalised people on stage and in media, as 'presentation is representation'. She offers presentation training to associations that support women, minorities, and marginalised people, to help level the business playing field.

If you would like to share your thoughts or stories about your own experiences with limiting beliefs such as Imposter Syndrome, you can do so on Lauren's website, where curated content from Imposter Syndrome sufferers is posted, or share excerpts at the contact points below. Any thoughts can be shared anonymously.

🌐 ImposterBook.com

📘 @ImposterBook

🐦 @ImposterBook

📷 @imposterlvalbert, using the hashtags #ImposterSyndrome and #ImposterBook